In My Father's Words

In My Father's Words

The World War II Letters of an Army Doctor

LAURA CANTOR ZELMAN

ISBN: 0692717293
ISBN 13: 9780692717295
Library of Congress Control Number: 2016908169
Laura Cantor Zelman, Potomac Falls, VA

Captain Milton Cantor, M.D.

This book is lovingly
dedicated to the memory of my parents
Milton and Rose Cantor.
May their lives stand as an example of honor, courage and service and to
their Grandchildren and Great-Grandchildren
May they always appreciate the sacrifices others made so that
they could enjoy the blessings of freedom.

Contents

Introduction

"Please keep my letters carefully from now on as someday, I really hope to complete a book (in diary form) about my experiences." Milton Cantor, January 7, 1942

"Perhaps in our old age we'll want to reread our correspondence." Milton Cantor, March 6, 1945

And so my Mother saved the 529 plus letters that my Dad wrote to her from January 1941 to July 1945 while serving in World War II as an Army doctor. My parents never did look at them again nor did my Dad ever write a book. Maybe they wanted to put those years behind them or maybe they were just too busy between my Dad's medical practice and raising four girls. My sisters and I found the letters in 1990 while clearing out their apartment. They were stuffed into bags, either loose or tied in bundles, in no particular order. I took the letters home and again they languished on a shelf while I was busy with my life.

Finally, in 2014, I decided to organize and read the letters. I was amazed at the quantity of them, the detailed descriptions of Dad's Army life and the emotions and longings expressed in the letters.

My Dad, Milton Cantor, was born in 1910 in Minsk, Russia. He was the youngest of eight children. In 1916 my Dad, his Mother, three sisters and a brother immigrated to the

United States. They joined their Father and older siblings who had finally saved enough money to pay for their passage.

America was truly the land of golden opportunity for my Dad. Even as a young boy his dream was to become a doctor. He studied hard and graduated from the City College of New York in 1932. Probably due to unwritten quotas for Jews, he could not gain admittance to an American medical school. Holding on to his dream, he applied to medical schools in Europe. He was accepted at the University of Graz in Austria. Since all the courses were taught in German, he had to master the language very quickly. His ability to speak German would prove to be a valuable asset during the war.

My Mom, Rose, met Dad in 1930. She encouraged his goal of becoming a doctor, even though it meant long periods of separation and loneliness for her. During his years studying in Graz, 1932-1937, they saw each other only when he returned home on summer break. I also have the numerous letters they wrote to each other during this time, but that is another story. Dad received his M.D. degree in 1937 and they were married in 1938.

Marital bliss would not be theirs for long. Another lengthy separation was on the horizon. While they were settling into married life, war clouds were gathering in Europe. Dad may have been in the Army Reserve as early as 1939. I cannot verify this as his records were amongst those destroyed in a fire at the National Personnel Records Center in 1973. His first letter home is dated January 26, 1941; the last letter is dated July 8, 1945.

Milton Cantor was a Husband, Father, Physician, American Patriot, Committed Jew and a Compassionate Human Being. He viewed himself as an ordinary man, honored to serve his country in order to preserve its freedoms. I hope the excerpts from his letters will convey the many facets of my Dad, an ordinary man who proudly did his best under extraordinary circumstances.

Working on my Dad's letters was a wonderful experience for me. Dad was 31 years old when he entered the Army. Through the letters I got to know my Dad as a young man in the prime of his life. As I read, it was as if I were right there with him experiencing all that he went through and all that he was thinking during his World War II Army service. The

*world of the 1940's was very different from the world we live in today. The letters gave me
a glimpse of that time. I felt that a unique gift had been given to me, my sisters and our
families. I believe these letters are a treasure to be shared.*

Laura Cantor Zelman

A Word About the Format

*I*t would have been impossible to include every letter and every word in each letter. Many of the letters are redundant because a lot of Dad's days were very routine. Therefore, I had to make choices as to what to include. If I left out words in the middle of a sentence, I indicated that by .... (ellipses). I did not indicate where I left out whole sentences or paragraphs.

My Father's words are in regular text. My comments are in Italics.

All the letters begin with Dearest Rose and end with variations of the word Love so I left the salutation and ending off all the letters.

I did not correct any spelling, punctuation or grammatical errors in the letters. They are as my Father wrote them.

For about a month in early 1942 Dad kept a diary. I thought it was important to use some of the writing from the diary. I have clearly indicated those excerpts taken from his diary and those from his letters.

One

*D*ad went into the Army in January, 1941, eleven months before the United States declared war. He was a Lieutenant in the Medical Corps. He was sent to Madison Barracks, New York first and then to Fort Dix, New Jersey. Both posts were not too far from Brooklyn, New York. Therefore, he was able to come home occasionally. After my birth, Dad rented a house near Madison Barracks. Mom and I joined him there. We were also able to join Dad when he was transferred to Fort Dix.

While Dad's life was now regimented, for the most part he adjusted to Army life quite well. One might say his first year in the Army was not too difficult. It appears that he thought his Army service would not last long. At this point, he could not have foreseen what the next few years would bring.

1st Lieutenant Milton Cantor and Rose
Madison Barracks, New York
1941

Captain Milton Cantor, M.D.   **Rose and Milton**

Two

January 26, 1941

I reached Watertown (*New York*) about 10 a.m. The weather was 25 degrees above. I didn't feel like waiting 1 ¼ hours for the next bus to Madison Barracks so I hired a taxi; latter cost $2 (distance of about 11 miles) which took me to headquarters.

After the preliminary introductions I was sent to the hospital for another physical exam… I was then sent to the finance officer where I reported my mileage and made arrangements for my pay. I was then assigned to quarters…

My quarters are comfortable, but crowded. Five of us live in a one family house and although we have steam heat, hot and cold running water and a bath-tub, we have only one toilet…. There are no quarters available for married people on the post (military grounds). These must be rented out of town.

The officers dine together in the officers' mess. The charge is $1 daily for 3 swell meals. We get plenty of fruits & vegetables, fine variety of foods & the cooking is excellent…

I didn't have to purchase any boots as the army rents galoshes free of charge. This I did and believe me it is very essential here. The snow just keeps accumulating & the wind blows it all over the place. The ground is so full of ice that I'm actually often forced to feel my way…

I'm assigned to the station hospital. Of course, the work is not as interesting as in a good hospital. However, the surroundings are pleasant and everyone tries to be nice towards each other.

I'm enclosing a ten dollar check to you. Make some financial arrangement with Ann (*the sister with whom she lived*). We are paid once a month… I reckon on sending you $60 monthly. If you need more, just let me know; if anything is left over bank it in your own name.

Gee! Honey, I miss you. I hope the months fly by.

February 3, 1941

As the days go rolling by I fall more and more into that military swing or the army way of doing things. In addition I get acquainted with more and more people and feel more at home…

The social life in any Army post is very important. A social visit to the homes of the commanding officers is almost mandatory and the visitor should excuse himself after a 20 minute visit, unless of course, the host insists (which is infrequently) on your staying. At any of the dances it is of prime importance to dance with the wife of your superior officer, at least once.

Last Saturday night a farewell dinner-dance was given in honor of the departing officers. Soldiers up to the grade of 2nd Lt. never mix socially with the higher officers; so that only 2nd Lts. & above with their female partners were invited… I danced with the wife of our Chief Med. Officer — although she's a Grandmother she's a swell dancer — and of course, danced with the wives of other officers. We all had a swell time… All were very friendly and courteous. Dress is either full military or tuxedo & gowns for the females. I guess I'll need my tuxedo up here as these affairs are run about twice monthly.

Our hours at the hospital are 8 a.m. – 4 p.m. We take turns being Officer of the Day which puts you on a 24 hr. duty. When you're on sick call duty you start the dispensary going at 7:30 a.m. We have Sat. & Sun. afternoons off, except of course, when you're the O.D. = officer of the day.

Although I miss you immensely I'm glad, in a certain way, you're not here. The grounds are so slippery as to make it absolutely dangerous for a woman in your condition (*pregnant with me, their first child*)…

February 15, 1941

Madison Barracks is like a little town with its own butcher & grocery store, fruit & vegetable store, tailor, barber, shoemaker & candy store. A haircut is 30 cents, men's rubber heels are 50 cents.

The Army has just forbidden the sale of liquors at Officers' Clubs. One can, if desired, buy alcoholic beverages, bring it to the club & drink it there or in his quarters. However, no such hard drinks will be on sale at Army posts throughout the good old U.S.A. This will enable the men to save some extra money.

March 9, 1941

Last Friday night I drove down to the Synagogue in Watertown. The Army furnishes free transportation to the soldiers & so every Friday night the trucks leave the post about 7:30 p.m. & drive straight to the Synagogue where the congregation waits for the soldiers to commence services.

At these services a few Jewish girls came down to meet the Army. I've been told that some "pious" romances are in the budding. Refreshments are often served. When the Christian boys heard about the women & food they also began to attend services.

The Protestant Chaplain here…also has attended the Hebrew services. He is a very fine gentleman who will help anyone. We all like him.

Since next week is Purim, a feast will be spread for the soldiers next Friday night in the Synagogue. One of the Jews has invited the officers to his home… We'll probably attend.

April 6, 1941

Tomorrow is Army Day and a parade is scheduled here. The post has invited the townspeople to inspect the grounds and witness the parade. Some of the Watertown socialites have been invited to dine with us and spend a social evening at the Officers' Club.

I'm trying to get away for the Passover holidays… I'll try hard to get leave.

Now that the grand event is very near (*my impending birth*) please take extra care of yourself. Don't go for long or even more than short walks. In other words, stick close to the house.

In the approaching happy days I'll be thinking of you & loving you constantly.
(*Dad was granted leave for the Passover holiday and was home when Mom went into labor. He was present and assisted at my birth.*)

May 18, 1941

I reached my destination (*returning to Madison Barracks after being home in Brooklyn, New York*) on a lovely spring day. It made my eyes gaze with joy at the magnificent scenery. What a different feeling one experiences gazing at natural beauty in contrast to artificial city splendors. All I needed to complete my blue heaven was baby & you.

Yesterday I was kept quite busy with a soldier who was suffering from a ruptured stomach ulcer. He was the most interesting surgical case we've had so far.

This morning I was on a board with 3 Majors to determine which applicants were to be sent to an officer's school. Our post was permitted 7 men; we had 12 applicants. The way we examined them reminded me of the intern examinations.

It's really lovely how these helpless babies sort of grow on you and become a "magnificent obsession." On the way to the train I kept thinking of little Laura. I kept on picturing her cute mimics and the way she kept her petite head on my shoulder…

--- even her cries would be welcome now.

Well honey, it looks pretty certain that we have a house here which pretty soon we'll turn into our "blue heaven". Until then I'll be anxiously waiting cause I miss you both.

May 23, 1941

I have good news for you. That little house I was telling you about is being vacated and will be turned over to us. It is a furnished house, also has a piano and consists of 3 rooms --- the parlor and kitchen on the ground floor and the bathroom and bedroom upstairs. I am looking for a refrigerator to rent.

A boat company which conducts tours of the 1000 Islands has invited 100 officers of the post to be their guests tomorrow afternoon for a sightseeing trip of the Islands… This free tour will therefore, be a very scenic one for us.

I'll probably be in the City during Decoration (*Memorial Day)* weekend so I'll be seeing you soon. Meanwhile, take good care of yourself as I know the baby is in perfect hands.

My Mother and I joined my Dad and lived in the little house near the Madison Barracks post from July to sometime in September. Dad was transferred to the 210th General Hospital, Fort Dix, New Jersey sometime around the end of September, 1941. Mom and I joined him in mid- October. He had rented an apartment for us in Bordentown, New Jersey.

October 1, 1941

Our O.D. schedule is in full swing and according to the schedule just posted, I'm on duty this weekend. I'm Administrative O.D. Saturday (Oct. 4) and Medical O.D. Sunday… I'll be off the following weekend and will therefore, be in Brooklyn.

From now on it'll be duty on every other weekend. I was Med. O.D. yesterday and must have walked about 3 miles during rounds even though I was fasting *(it was Yom Kippur)*. Today I went into Trenton to attend services and after that began to look around for apartments.

I moved out of the tent & got temporary quarters in the hospital. The rooms are quite comfortable.

Dad departed Fort Dix on January 6, 1942. He did not know where he was headed. Mom and I returned to Brooklyn, New York. We lived with my Aunt Ann, Uncle Lou and their children. On December 7, 1941 Japan bombed Pearl Harbor, Hawaii and the United States entered World War II against Japan, Germany and Italy.

Three

*T*he night before his departure from Fort Dix Dad started a diary. He kept it for about one month. Initially he didn't know where he was headed nor when or if he would see us again. This is an excerpt from his January 5, 1942 entry:

Although I didn't wish to, Rose insisted that I read the outline of my parting message to Laura. I read it to her in bed and she began to cry bitterly. I omitted reading the paragraph beginning with "If it is my fate to make the supreme sacrifice". I knew if I read that it would almost cause as much commotion as a funeral. Rose and I then began to sort of apologize to each other for some of our tempers & tantrums. I guess such a departure makes a person repent & see the good in others. Thought about the baby & how I'd miss her, especially her cute antics "I see you – bye bye – and clap hands".

The parting letter that my Dad wrote was presented to me on my eighteenth birthday. Thankfully, he was there to give it to me. It was in an envelope that was well sealed with tape. The envelope was marked "To – Laura Ellen Cantor from Dad – to be opened & read by her April 12, 1959". Inside was a three-page handwritten letter:

Jan. 7, 1942

On the train in Indiana

Dearest little Laura,

I was present and assisted at your birth. I even was watching over your Mother during her labor ordeal. Like all Mothers, she had to suffer much to bring into this world your "tender little form".

After your birth we were very happy. I only had 4 days leave from the Army, having been called to serve Uncle Sam Jan. 23, 1941. When my leave was terminated I had to return to duty; thereby denying to your Mother that which a woman most cherishes, the presence of her husband during the trying childbirth days.

Every time I could get away, I hurried down to Brooklyn to see Mother and you.

Each time you "just grew on me" and became so dear to me that I began to miss you.

How happy I was when your Mother and you were able to join me July 2, 1941 to make our home at my post, Madison Barracks, N.Y.

Now dearest little Laura you're "everything in the world to me". My heart is heavy; when I think of leaving you it becomes even heavier.

War is now on and my outfit, the 210th General Hospital, has been ordered to a secret destination. Please remember that your daddy is proud to serve this great land of liberty, the U.S.A.

Even though I feel sadly in leaving Mother and you, I'm glad to do my little share.

If the Lord spares me I hope to return and spend many happy days with Mother and you. If it shall be my fate to make the supreme sacrifice, I shall pray for you wherever I'll be.

I love you dearly and know that you'll always take care of your Mother whom I've loved. I trust and pray that your life and character will be modeled after that of your Mother.

May your life be as bright and as successful as I would have tried to make it.

Wherever you'll be I'll pray for and guard over you.

My only parting message is to follow that from the "Golden Book"

"Do unto others as you would have others do unto you."

Daddy

Four

I thought it was important to use some of the writing from Dad's diary. I have clearly indicated those excerpts taken from his diary and those from his letters.

January 6, 1942
From the Diary

Awoke early & settled some of the last minute affairs... Picked up baby & hugged her, didn't say anything out loud for fear my voice would crack. Glad that baby was too young to understand. In my heart I wondered whether I'd ever see her again... Laura was taken to the window, Rose & Mother accompanied me to the R.R. station at Dix. It was freezing weather. At the station met the other officers who were glad to notice the big salami I had wrapped up... Last minute instructions from Mother "Watch yourself – write often". Finally the tearful & painful parting... Rose & Mother carried on exceedingly well despite their heavy hearts...

Our own kitchen did the cooking & feeding for the 120 nurses, 75 officers & 30 soldiers.

January 7, 1942

From the Diary

Didn't sleep so well in my upper berth last night. We sang, told jokes & stories, read or played cards & chess to while time away. Wrote my message to Laura which is to be opened by her & read on her 18th birthday... Boys in good spirits. I guess it was the "laugh clown laugh act". Thought of baby, Rose, Mother, of family.

January 7, 1942

From a Letter

This letter is being written on the train speeding through Indiana...

We are fed by our own kitchen and the dining system is a good one. We remain in our original seats. The soldiers then come around & hand each of us a knife, fork and spoon – other soldiers then follow in quick succession with paper plates, paper cups and napkins. Then comes bread (2 slices white), slab of butter and after that 2 soldiers carry in big pots of meat, potatoes, string beans, gravy & coffee...

Last night I started the salami and in a short time it was devoured; we got bread from our kitchen.

Incidentally, I forgot to give you the power of attorney forms which are all filled out. You'll find them in the desk... Put these papers in a vault along with the others.

While the train was moving I rewrote my little message to the baby. I am enclosing it. It is my express desire and wish that Laura should be the first one to open it & read it on her 18th birthday – so also place it in the vault together with my insurance policies, etc.

Please keep my letters carefully from now on as someday, I really hope to complete a book (in diary form) about my experiences.

January 8, 1942
From the Diary

Breakfast at 9 a.m. consisting of 2 slices bread & butter, 2 hard-boiled eggs, bacon, cocoa & an orange – by this time we were passing thru Mississippi & saw no snow—crossed then into LA & arrived at New Orleans at 12:30 p.m. Were then shifted to the wharf… Red Cross volunteers came on the wharf with coffee, cookies, cigarettes & took our letters (without stamps) to mail. New Orleans newspaper took our picture on the train while taking tin cup of coffee from the Red Cross – after much fuss about baggage we were given our stateroom numbers & boarded the boat. Were given new gas masks as we started on the gangplank – boat was painted battleship gray & was the 15 yr. old SS "Shawnee" of the Cuban Mail Line… boat normally accommodated 500, now had over 1800 soldiers & officers on board. Blackout on deck from sunset to sunrise – no smoking on deck. It is quite evident that we are not being convoyed.

We now know that we are headed for the Canal Zone… Whether we'll stay in the Canal Zone or continue to some other destination is a question. Everybody jokes & walks thru corridors – all hope we'll reach the Canal Zone safe. No one allowed on blacked out deck without wearing a life preserver.

January 9, 1942
From the Diary

Warmer today, comfortable on deck in blouse – sailing rougher, quite a few people seasick, fire drill today at 4 p.m. At sounding of bells we had to go to our respective lifeboats on "B" deck… Complete blackout after sunset – all portholes which are painted black must be closed. Fresh (faucet) water only turned on following hrs. 6:30-8:30 a.m., 11:30-1 p.m., 5-7 p.m. We continue to joke & seek company as this keeps one's mind occupied – learned how to play Rummy.

January 10, 1942
From the Diary

Very warm & smooth sailing – Caribbean Sea appears blue. Wore khaki & perspired much. It rained for a few minutes & then the sun would shine — this occurred 4 times. Some people were sun burned…

No radios permitted to be played. No hot water – was able to take a cold shower during time water was turned on. Since leaving New Orleans no news about the war…

The nurses especially should be given much credit. Though we all know that we are in danger all the time we all try to be cheerful. Often think of baby with her cute antics – wonder about Rose & Mother?

January 11, 1942
From the Diary

Very sunny & warm day – longed to be in a bathing suit. Got quite a sunburn of the face & neck. We were allowed to go without a necktie & with open collar, except for the night meal…

It was very cool & enjoyable on the blacked-out deck. At 10 p.m. we had to leave the deck & allowed to play cards, etc, in the dining room till 11 p.m. The latter was a hot box & we sweltered there… We all feel much safer now as we are approaching Cristobal (Colon) & we won't dock there until next morning – ship proceeding very slowly. We still don't know where our final destination will be… To bed at 11:30 p.m. in a hot room. We put all lights out & opened the portholes – what relief!

Five

*D*ad was now far from the cold and snow of winter, but the Panama Canal Zone was not exactly a tropical paradise. Dad settled into life at Fort Gulick as he helped to establish a permanent hospital there. While the real enemies were still far away, the tropics had its own kinds of antagonists. The soldiers there had to deal with heat, humidity, torrential downpours, mosquitoes, sandflies and malaria to name a few annoyances.

The letters express how much Dad missed his family, especially my Mother and me. However, no matter how lonely he was, he was proud to be doing his part to defend the U.S.A. He understood that all must sacrifice to make this world a better place. I can only imagine how lonely my Mother was as I read my Dad's efforts to keep her spirits up.

I think gradually Dad realized that this war would be tougher and last longer than he originally thought. He and his buddies made the best of the situation. They supported one another and laughed together; lasting friendships were made. The local Jewish residents opened their homes and their hearts to the soldiers.

I noticed that Dad used the plural "we" when writing about thoughts and feelings --- a testament to the camaraderie he shared with his fellow officers.

What an eye opening experience it must have been for someone from New York City to live and work in Panama in 1942. Dad loved to learn and seemed to enjoy studying Spanish and learning about the native culture.

Milton Cantor in Panama, 1942   **Laura in Kimono**
Dad Sent

Six

January 12, 1942

From the Diary

Docked at 9 a.m. At 10:30 we were allowed to leave the ship & wait inside the cool & enclosed pier. We walked outside the pier to waiting trucks – 12 officers to a truck – the nurses had remained on ship. We were then taken about 4 miles to Fort Gulick. On the pier we had heard from some officers about the fine setup for us at the Fort & we were certainly not disappointed...

We gazed in amazement as we noticed the imposing, spacious, numerous & concrete buildings we were to occupy. It acted like a rapid stimulant & tonic to us. What a contrast to Dix. Here all buildings are of concrete; they must be for otherwise the termites will in time destroy buildings built of wood. In addition the foundations rise about 7 feet from the ground. There are no glass windows, only screens which bring the welcomed wind. For lunch we were taken to Margarita which is the U.S. Government Civilian Employees settlement. Here we had a good meal & mailed some air mail letters home. Here we also spoke to some of the American residents who....invited us to their home.

January 12, 1942
From a Letter

Well, here we are safe & sound, healthy & hearty after a 4 day ocean trip. Now our address is no more censored. We are at Fort Gulick, Panama Canal, on the Atlantic side and are all happy. In my next letter I'll write everything. I merely wanted you to know that we are on terra firma & like the place.

January 13, 1942
From the Diary

Rained twice today & at times was very hot. I was O.D. & was taught the rudiments of how to use a 45 caliber pistol. Took a long walk & saw the excellent concrete family homes, the new station (400 beds) hospital in construction & the Gatun Lake. Spoke to one of the construction men here. He told me that the rainy season is May-Dec., that it rains twice as much on the Atlantic as on the Pacific side – that the land for Fort Gulick was surveyed beginning Sept. 10, 1939 – that construction of the buildings was begun April 1940.

We had a meeting at 8 p.m. & were told what to do in case of air raids. The only constructed air raid shelter here is beneath the soldier's mess hall. We were also ordered to be in our quarters by 11 p.m.

January 15, 1942
From the Diary

Was assigned to a gen. medicine ward. Our med. Chief asked us to draw up a ward plan. We got together, decided on a plan of action which was approved…

We had our first gas mask demonstration & drill & were required to march around for 10 min. with helmets & gas masks on. This was done to get us accustomed to wearing the mask.

As Assistant Infirmary O.D. I took care of 2 cases which appeared to have symptoms of heat exhaustion. The days are quite hot, but since we're not in the field we must wear a tie. A cool shower is only refreshing for about 1 hour & then you recommence to perspire freely & all your clothing again begins to feel wet. Mosquitoes don't seem to bother us much, but the tiny sandflies do; they creep in thru the screen mesh & bite. Went to the P.R. movies on the post. The lobby was a hotbed, but the theatre proper was very cool. Saw the "Maltese Falcon" --- admission 15 cents.

January 16, 1942
From the Diary

Spent the day visiting my ward which is being filled with 30 beds.

We had an officer's meeting…, were told about mail censorship & were carefully warned about naming installations or distances in our letters. Tomorrow we are to begin our own mess. The nurses are also to have their own separate mess.

Wish we didn't have to wear neckties & button our collars for when it's hot here, & it often is, it's annoying. We are trying to arrange Hebrew services. Signed up for the Spanish course. Blackout at 11 p.m. Lay awake for over an hour thinking of baby, Rose & Mother.

January 17, 1942
From the Diary

During the early morning hours it stormed for quite a while. It is very fortunate that most of our roads are paved. We are tickled pink that we have such fine toilets, 12 sinks with hot & cold running water & excellent showers with special footbaths, one on either end for the calcium hypochlorite solution.

We assembled for a meeting & were introduced to & addressed by… the Department Surgeon. He told us that we were to staff & man a permanent (at least for the duration of the war) hospital. Lunched at noon after which Skura, Robin & I walked down to the Margarita settlement.   It was a very hot day & we perspired freely. Much traffic on the way… Took haircuts & were told by the Puerto Rican barber that January is the coolest month of the year… At 8:30 p.m. about 40 of us assembled for the Spanish class. We are to have 2 lessons per week of 1 hour each.

January 18, 1942
From the Diary

At 8 p.m. nine other officers & I left for the M.P. tour of Colon. At the M.P. Headquarters we met Capt. Cummins who talked about the functions of the M.P.s & the off limit areas. He led us on foot thru some of these areas – one cabaret we visited had quite a foul stench & was full of soldiers, sailors & hostesses. We then walked thru the licensed Red light district where the prostitutes are examined weekly & must have a health card. These women sit or stand in front of their one room door. The 2nd floors are "Off Limits".

January 22, 1942
From the Diary

Last night Rabbi Witkin came down & held services for us. About 11 officers & 30 soldiers turned out. I soon recognized Rabbi Witkin as a former Young Israelite of Manhattan & we knew quite a few people in common. He told me he travels throughout Panama, Trinidad, Dutch Guinea. He was quite interesting & made a very favorable impression on us. At next Wednesday's services we are to have a "kosher salami" party.

January 23, 1942
From the Diary

Was told by…our Medical Chief to get our ward ready to receive patients by tomorrow. I …went to the supply section who promised me that they'd try to supply our ward. At 10 a.m.…was told to be ready to receive patients by 3 p.m. today. I therefore gathered the nurses, gave them a brief outline of our plans, drew up additional requirements & got in touch with the supply section again. By loaning them my ward men I was able to accelerate delivery. I then went to the infirmary, acquainted myself with the 4 patients…., returned to the ward and made arrangements with the dietitian for patients' meals.

Soon the equipment began to roll in. It really was a shame to see how the new and expensive equipment was damaged in shipment. I'm sure that a private party would refuse to accept such damaged articles. The pajamas & bathrobes were woolen & much too warm for the tropics. I was promised light clothing if available.

January 25, 26, 1942
From a Letter

Your first letter postmarked Brooklyn, Jan. 21 was received by me the morning of the 24th. I noticed that you used 15 cents worth of stamps. That won't be necessary anymore as the rates have been reduced both ways to 6 cents for ½ ounce. An ordinary brief might take 2 weeks to reach me. By spending 3 cents extra for airmail the letter arrives here in 2-4 days.

Although it's supposed to be the dry season now, it rains often and at times storms violently. They tell me that during the rainy season, May to December, it may pour continuously for 10 days. That's when my boots will come in handy.

I've already made the acquaintance of 2 Jewish families. They told me that there are 2 synagogues in town. As soon as I get a chance I shall visit them. These Jews were very friendly and opened their homes to us.

Through one of the Jewish residents of the town we contacted the only Rabbi who works for the Army & JWB (Jewish Welfare Board). We made arrangements to hold Hebrew services every Wednesday evening.

Our Spanish class is coming along slowly. Most of the natives speak English to a certain extent so that it's pretty hard to learn the language by conversation.

In a few days you should be receiving the January allotment. In case you can't manage, let me know & I'll try to send a few dollars from here.

January 26, 1942
From the Diary

After breakfast went to my ward, made rounds and then discussed with Maj. Bruton the laundry problem for the ward, the partitioning of the latrine so that the nurses may have some privacy, the disposal of waste material, etc. Then went to the supply section and requested additional supplies & equipment.

Upon my return to the barracks I was informed that 10 of us, I included, are to make the trip to Gorgas tomorrow. We are to breakfast at 6:15 a.m. & board the train for Panama City at 7 a.m.

January 27, 1942
From the Diary

After breakfast we were driven to the station. After arriving at Balboa all 10 of us piled into a 7 passenger taxi at 15 cents per & were driven to the Gorgas

Hospital. We were assigned to visit wards corresponding to our fields. I was taken to the Medical Ward & shown the cases of which 50% were Malaria. The ward was crowded with beds in the corridors.

This visit to Gorgas emphasized on us the importance of Malaria. Any fever case here should make us Malaria wise. Gorgas visit very valuable.

January 31, 1942
From the Diary

Bright, warm & clammy day with an occasional sprinkle. Worked in the ward & in the Dietetic Department. Just before lunch went to see about mail & found orders appointing me dietetic advisor to the Mess Officer in addition to my other duties – began to make mental plans about organizing the Special Diet Department. Got my pay check ($97.20) for Jan. Went to the post movies in the evening & later revisited the ward.

Those darn minute sandflies bite like the dickens. In addition one perspires freely with so little effort that you become listless & tire easily --- tropical effects.

February 1, 1942
From the Diary

Day hot and humid. Spent the morning in the Dietetic Department. In the afternoon a few of us went swimming in the Hotel Washington pool. We returned to the Fort for supper after which Cohen and I took a walk. Halfway up the hill, we noticed a continuous procession of ants. Those crawling with pieces of leaves (each ant pulled a ½" square leaf) went in one direction while those returning empty- handed crawled in another direction. Each line stretched for many yards. It was remarkable to behold such a sight, so instinctively organized.

In the evening.....did our Spanish lessons. Then I went down to the Officers Club and wrote 2 letters.

Our Club is functioning – we bought furniture & opened a small bar.

February 1, 1942
From a Letter

Now we are supposed to have the dry season, but it rains plenty; three days ago it rained almost continuously, at times in torrents. Even though we have paved roads, the trucks & autos bring the mud so that boots come in very handy.

Interesting are the various signs one sees here as "For Gold patients only" or "For Silver patients". Upon inquiring I was told that this nomenclature dates back to the building of the Canal when the American White employees were paid in gold and the Negro and others (Indians, "white trash") were paid in silver; so that in essence it means for white or colored patients.

The color line here is strictly drawn, be it on trains, etc. I understand that the use of the drug marihuana is quite prevalent here amongst the Negroes and Indians.

On Wed. evening the Rabbi came down and brought plenty of salami and the Pitkin Ave. *(Brooklyn, N.Y.)* type of rye bread, also sour pickles. We supplied mustard, beer and coca colas. After the condensed Hebrew and English Services we had a swell feast. Many other faiths participated. Both the Catholic and Protestant Chaplains, the Colonel, etc. were present.

The Rabbi also brought down with him some Jewish residents and promised us a monthly feast. That salami tasted swell.

There is very little farming in Panama. Most of the vegetables are imported from the U.S.A. We wouldn't dare buy vegetables from the few local native farmers. They use all kinds of animal excreta for the fertilizers. Diseases like dysentery, typhoid fever, cholera, etc. can thus be easily spread. The Army therefore never purchases any local vegetables.

Jan. 30th was the Presidents' birthday ball. Tickets were sold at $1 per couple and the affair was held at the Stranger's Club. Those of us who could get away attended this worthy (cause) event. I believe that over $1000 was raised for the Infantile Paralysis fund.

I expect to be quite busy for the next few weeks with the Dietetic Department and also with the investigation of a fever currently here. We get off one afternoon a week and one evening (curfew at 11 p.m.).

If you give me an idea of your expenditures I'd know whether I can also buy some government bonds, otherwise as per our conversation I'll send some money to you.... I insist that you don't stint. Whatever clothing you need get some. Try to save for we'll need dinero when it's over…

I don't think a day passes when I don't picture "little Honey" and you. I guess if she were here she'd make us all happier. What's the use of dwelling on this subject, it only makes me lonesome.

February 3, 1942
From the Diary

Worked out standard diet forms & drew up a plan of operation --- submitted same to Maj. Bruton for approval which was granted. In a fervent discussion I let Lt.... know that I've been appointed Dietetic Advisor and not Assistant Mess Officer.

Am getting accustomed to the taste of the local water. Paid mess bill for 19 days in Jan. ---was $19.35

Since it was a clear, full moon night we walked around the Fort & had an interesting discussion about the Army for over an hour. We all felt that the opinions of the junior officers should be sought out & encouraged.

The Diary ends here. No reason is given. All further excerpts will be from letters.

February 8, 1942

I received your letter dated the 30th of Jan. and was very glad to hear so much about "the apple of my eye".

Your fine descriptions of "little Honey" really thrill me. I often reread each such paragraph 2 – 3 times. Incidentally, what I now miss I can make up in films. Suppose you make an arrangement with Lou to take movies every 2 – 3 months and of course you pay for the films. In this way I'll be able to watch her "grow-up".

In addition to mosquitoes, there are the tiny sandflies. These are so tiny that they creep through our tiny screens; and do they bite! Some of our personnel have had to be admitted to the hospital for severe bites with secondary infections due to scratching.

At least the mosquitoes are for the most part kept out by the screens and one has to watch himself when out in the open after sundown. None of our buildings here have windows, only screens and I've been bitten quite a few times by these pesty sandflies.

Malaria is quite prevalent here and we are constantly on the lookout for same at the hospital. Every fever case is a potential Malaria case and precautions are taken until proven otherwise.

My Special Diets Department is functioning quite well. The hospital itself is beginning to run smoothly and we are getting more and more patients. Tropical medicine is in many respects so different that it's very interesting, at least to doctors, to watch the course of events.

Again the censors have changed their minds. Now we are required to write the name of our unit on the envelope.

The cost of living here is quite high. Every item is more expensive than in the states. Give me the good old U.S.A. for mass production prices.

As I write airplanes are patrolling overhead. The jungle looks very peaceful. We are on the alert however and when possible enjoy ourselves as best we can.

One of the boys has a short wave radio so that we get news daily. The newspapers here are half English and half Spanish. On Sundays the comics, which are those as presented in the "Daily News" appear in Spanish – little orphan Annie has suddenly become a linguist.

February 15, 1942

I received yours and baby's valentines simultaneously and was really thrilled. It was very thoughtful of you. I want you to know that even though I may not say it in all my letters, a day never passes without my thinking of my two lovely ladies.

In addition, as you can gather, you can't say too much. All the mail passes thru the censors where often the mail is delayed… Therefore, don't be surprised if you don't always receive weekly mail. It just can't be helped.

We've just moved to our new quarters. Two officers are assigned to a house which would be ideal for "our blue heaven". These houses were built in peace time for the families of the non-commissioned officers. They've been turned over to us and are grand.

The first night spent in my new abode was a sleepless one. Believe it or not the sandfleas, mosquitoes, flies, etc. even attacked "a sour-puss" like me and when these tiny sandfleas bite your ancestors feel it too. Now I have a very fine net which is so fine that it almost keeps the air out too. It does the trick though and I can at least rest in peace.

February 22, 1942

The hospital is running smoothly and we are getting our share of Malaria cases. We are on a 7 day schedule and to break the monotony are lucky to be able to have a dance once in a while.

Last Tuesday evening the Gorgas Hospital had talks on Malaria. We arrived there an hour early so another officer & I phoned our Chaplain, Rabbi Witkin, who drove down to the station and took us to his home which is in the U.S.O. building operated by the JWB (Jewish Welfare Board).

The JWB have thrown their doors open to service men of all faiths. Here the soldiers can read, write, play pool, ping pong, etc., take showers & get free towels & soap. A gym is also provided.

We were then driven to Gorgas Hospital where we attended the most interesting talks and returned later to Fort Gulick. These lectures are of inestimable help to us in treating Malaria.

At our Wednesday evening service Rabbi Witkin invited us to the Passover Seder. The first one will be held on the Pacific side and the second one on the Atlantic side. All officers and soldiers are invited and there is absolutely no charge. The JWB is footing all bills.

A Jewish family in town has invited about 15 Jewish officers, including myself, to the first Seder. Mighty nice of them and if possible, I'll be glad to attend.

I'm enclosing a money order for fifty dollars. Twenty five dollars is a birthday gift and twenty five an anniversary gift…. I'd like you to buy for yourself anything you desire or need. I hope and pray that our fifth anniversary will be spent together.

March 1, 1942

I'm very glad that you are not alone this year. At least there's a most precious tot to occupy your time, to divert your mind, to soothe your emotions and to give vent to your feelings. I do hope and pray that next year we'll all be together.

I wish we had some of your cold weather. One hot day after another is no comfort and in addition there's the insects to contend with. Sometimes we even wish we were in Iceland.

March 10, 1942

During last night it rained so that this morning I had to wear my boots to get down to the Mess Hall. Some areas really become puddles so that after the rain the Sanitation Squads must squirt an anti-mosquito breeding liquid into such stagnant rain water. Otherwise the Malaria producing mosquitoes will multiply tremendously.

The beginning and the end of the rainy season always increase the malarial rates… Rainfall increases the breeding places of these pests. There's so much jungle space here that the control problem becomes colossal.

There are many other cases you seldom see in the good old U.S.A. The tropics produce its own brand of medicine.

Our ward work is therefore quite interesting and in the short space of time we've been here we've done quite a good setup job. My ward is almost filled to capacity.

Most of the boys here are at a loss, after a while, as to what to write. For a while after our arrival we were able to describe the towns, natives & some of the scenery. Now, after you've done all that, you must pause & reflect.

To write interesting things and those the home people would like to read would not only be censored, but would undoubtedly aid the enemy.

Therefore, if my letters become dull don't blame me. All I can say is we're on duty most of the time, on the alert and ready.

I'm feeling all right and as I've often repeated before, a day doesn't pass without thinking of you & baby. I often imagine her "antics" which sort of brighten the hours. Sometimes I think of Bordentown & the pleasant days there. I know there must be silver linings behind those very dark clouds, and someday the sun will shine again, and people will be let alone to live as they see fit.

March 14, 1942

I've got some good news. We have been made to understand that a 10% increase in salary has been granted us, effective from the date we left the continental U.S. That means that 10% of your base pay or for me of $166.67. That $16.66 extra each month will certainly come in handy as it's just a little less than my monthly insurance cost. As soon as we get it I'll allot same to you…

March 23, 1942

I've just received your letter and noting its weight judged it to contain the pictures…

If someone handed me some of these pictures at random, I wouldn't recognize my daughter. She's changed quite a bit since Jan. 12th… Her smile melted even my "soldier's heart". Boy! I sure would like to see and hold her even for a few minutes.

It's so humid, warm and uncomfortable here that I just can't bring myself to write to anyone else except you and Mother. At night it's almost impossible to sit in your house, read or write. These darn sandfleas sting the hell out of you.

It seems that everybody else can enjoy their husbands while yours is serving our V cause. Well honey, if it weren't for sacrifices our country would be lost and to me she's worth anything I may be asked to do.

March 31, 1942

The censors are so tight now that one is limited on almost everything except personal or family problems. To write to others therefore is truly a dull task.

A few days ago a most welcome regulation was issued so that now we don't have to wear ties on the post. The closed collar and tie certainly made it uncomfortable, especially during the hot hours. When we leave the post we must wear a tie.

April 3, 1942

The Seders came and went and happy to see we were not forgotten – thanks to the Jewish Welfare Board and to the many spirited local Jewish residents.

The first Seder was held in the house of the Gorin family who had invited about 35 soldiers, sailors and the 3 Jewish nurses. There was gefilte fish, roast chicken and all the other Pesach delicacies. The Haggadah was read… Only wine was scarce as it is difficult to obtain…

Last night the second Seder was held. This was sponsored by the Jewish Welfare Board who also were the hosts for the first Seder held on the Pacific side. I was informed that over 500 men attended…while about 300 participated in the second.

Matzohs were also passed out to those boys who wanted it for the entire Passover. I got a few pounds and will certainly abstain from bread for the duration of the holiday.

April 8, 1942

Oh! I almost forgot. Far be it from me to deprive the 210th Auxiliary from anything of interest. With my compliments please report at your next meeting that we now dine with the nurses instead of separately, as before. I'm sure the Ladies Auxiliary will be able to build up from this humble scrap.

I've just finished reading a most interesting, sensational and fascinating book called "Total Espionage" by Curt Riess. It's the story of the entire spy system of Nazi Germany, Japan, England and France. Its revelations are hair-raising. It's very easy to understand exactly why France fell, who the actual French traitors were…

Well I've finished the letter, but I'll never finish loving you & baby and missing you. A day never passes without thinking of you two or wishing I could be with you.

I'm still & always will be happy in the thought that I'm doing my bit – no matter what the cost. I shall always strive to defend free America.

April 11, 1942

I can just imagine my "little honey" walking. Sometimes I close my eyes, relax and image baby walking towards my outstretched arms. When I think of her, I'm more than anxious to do my bit towards making this world a decent place for her to dwell in.

Incidentally your last letter was examined by the censor and left intact, including little Laura's picture.

With our short wave radios made especially for the tropics we get some fine broadcasts from the states. It's a tribute to the U.S.A. that it trusts its citizens to listen to all kinds of radio programs, even foreign broadcasts.

The sneaky fascists have a death penalty for listening to foreign broadcasts. This fact alone proves how the dictators fear to have their subjects…know the truth. All of us here will defend Uncle Sam with zeal, enthusiasm, vigor and vim. It may take us a little time to prepare, but when we'll strike it'll be a mighty victorious force that just won't and can't be stopped.

April 12, 1942

So far today I've just had one thought in mind. As a matter of fact, as soon as I opened my eyes this morning it obsessed me. Yes, you've guessed it, the first anniversary of the birth of our "little daughter".

I'll be thinking today of my "little honey" and wish her many, many happy years.

April 16, 1942

Life goes on as usual. Since only five of us remain in the Spanish class, we've cut down the sessions to once per week. The other way it would have been too expensive, $2 apiece per week.

The rainy season is almost here. There is less sun and more clouds now and it often pours like hell.

We take turns censoring the soldier's mail. Many have left wives and sweethearts behind. Yes, you're right; almost everyone is making a sacrifice. By the way, what do girls do for dates now?

It just started to rain like blazes. It's only the beginning. They tell me "you ain't seen nothing yet." May is supposed to be the worst weather month here with a most uncomfortable humidity. We perspire so much that we take extra portions of salt.

April 24, 1942

Last Monday we began Pop's yahrzeit *(the anniversary of his Father's death)*. I assembled ten officers for a minyon and was therefore able to say Kaddish.

It's remarkable how many items turn moldy. Books, leather goods, shoes & woolens will absolutely turn moldy if not kept dry (in a heated closet) and if not brushed frequently. I applied an insect repellent to my book covers; the insects were repelled, but mold was all over. Everything susceptible to molds must be kept dried, aired and dusted frequently.

The package that Mother sent me contained a Manischewitz cake wrapped in a cellophane box. It took 2 weeks to reach me and upon examining the cake and cutting it the mold was quite evident so it went into the garbage. The egg matzohs, halvah, figs, plums & candy were ok. The salami was also ok after a little treatment.

In addition to my medical duties and head of the Special Diet Division, I'm now also appointed Food and Nutrition Officer where I get to serve in an advisory and consulting capacity.

There's so much mud that my zipper shoes come in very handy. Those of us who neglected to buy them in the states are now very sorry and offer to buy same, but there are no sellers.

The weather has been put on the censor's list so that's another item to strike off.

May 17, 1942

I'm busy now working on the plans and duties of a Food and Nutrition Officer. I have to submit monthly reports to the Surgeon General in Washington, thru channels... on the nutritional status of our troops.

This is in addition to my ward duties and to my duties as Director of the Special Diets in the Hospital. Food has always been a ticklish problem in any army. Imagine trying to keep a young soldier with stomach complaints on a diet.

I have an interest in dietetics and nutrition and that is probably the reason I was picked for the job. Everything is ok except those monthly reports which require a lot of work and investigation.

It's now reached the stage where we can sit in our quarters, take our shirts off and enjoy it without fearing the sandfly. I don't know whether this will be permanent, but it'll be paradise while it lasts.

I read about the gasoline rationing. It seems that many people will do a lot of walking from now on…

May 20, 1942

Yesterday was "Bond Day" at Fort Gulick and an attempt was made to get all the officers and soldiers to buy war bonds on an allotment basis. Of course all this was voluntary and absolutely no compulsion was or will be used. A private soldier earning the Canal Zone minimum of $40 monthly could allot a minimum of $1.25 per month. When the $18.75 has been paid he receives a $25 bond. The minimum an officer may allot is $3.75.

From the $77 I receive here monthly, I've allotted $6.25. Therefore, every three months, when the total of $18.75 has been reached a $25 bond will be mailed…

In addition, sometimes buy bonds with the surplus cash you might have on hand. They'll be an excellent source of saving and we'll be carrying out a patriotic duty. Actually by helping Uncle Sam, we'll be helping ourselves.

Our short wave radios give us all the news from the states. We were all tickled pink to learn the results of the Coral Sea battle. Boy! When our men have the necessary equipment and numbers they're tops.

May 24, 1942

The USO is certainly trying to make the soldiers happier and more content. An office has been opened in town advising us where and how to spend time in the city, where to eat and other related information.

In my last week's afternoon off George and I went to town for a swim. Fortunately we had a little sun and got tanned. Everything felt so peaceful in those waters; it almost felt like a dream world.

I understand that Rabbi Witkin will return here shortly. In the interim we continue services once a week with either myself or some of the soldiers as the conductor. On Shevuoth, a few of us gathered in the chapel to say Yizkor.

How are you set on money now? Can you manage well on the $166 monthly? Let me know how things stand.

May 30, 1942

This was one of the busiest weeks I have spent here. I had a very busy O.D.... There was plenty of work on the ward and in addition, I had to write 2 articles – a monthly nutrition report and an article on Food and Health.

Our unit publishes a weekly newspaper which is edited & staffed by our soldiers. To instruct the men in the fundamentals of nutrition, I have decided to run a weekly column called "Food and Nutrition". This is entirely voluntary on my part. Even if it is not instructive, it'll help the editors to fill some space… I am also holding weekly conferences with the Mess Committee in an attempt to improve the mess situation. At least when you're busy the time passes rapidly.

A few nights ago I saw "How Green Was My Valley" on the post. I enjoyed it immensely. One can't realize what a morale lifter movies can be. Whenever a certain locality in the U.S. is mentioned or flashed on the screen its partisans cheer.

This Sunday 3 others and I have been invited to a borscht meal. Our hosts will be Mr. & Mrs. Schwartz. Already our mouths our watering.

I often think of Bordentown. Somehow that place took a hold in my memory. Maybe because we had a "blue heaven" there. When I return we'll make it a "red- letter day."

So keep your chin up gal. Remember that our Victory is worth any sacrifice. Also remember that your soldier boy is proud of his uniform, proud of Uncle Sam and proud to do his bit.

May 30, 1942
7:30 p.m.

This is to inform you that you are no longer the wife of Lt. Milton Cantor. From now on you shall be the spouse of Captain Milton Cantor… It happened about an hour ago when a group of us took the oath of office of our new ranks.

I first heard about my promotion when I entered the mess hall. One of the nurses congratulated me. I asked her for what, and she replied "on becoming a captain". I replied that April fool was sixty days ago.

You can't censure me for the latter statement. Promotions were slow in coming; in fact, so slow that some of us despaired of ever being advanced. When therefore, 13 promotions reached our headquarters today the alarm was given. I hadn't heard of it and thought that the nurse's remarks were a gag.

Of course, some were quite disappointed in not receiving a promotion. My 16 months of service made me the second oldest 1st Lt. in point of service.

As soon as I get a chance I'll increase your allotment from $166 to $203.33.

Actually my pay increase will be $56.66 per month. If you want we can put it into bonds. Let me know your opinion.

June 28, 1942

New regulations have been issued by the censors. Effective July 1st we are to change our address as follows:

Capt. Milton Cantor, M.C. 210 General Hospital
A.P.O. 837, c/o Postmaster New Orleans, La.

The reason is obvious. Even in your letters you must not make statements or ask questions concerning my location or give any hints. This is a military order which must be implicitly obeyed. We will also use U.S. stamps henceforth.

I'm glad you're finally settled in the country *(for the summer in upstate New York)*... Now that you're settled and all's well, I'll write more often. Especially these days do I think of you and baby. Many times our lives pass in review and I feel remorseful when I think of your married life; and now when a "little angel" has arrived the "big devil" has to be away.

I do love you darling and miss you very much. The tropics make you yearn for a lot of things and people. My whole present existence is for you and baby. I know that when this mess is over, you'll be there and we shall build a real "blue heaven" forever.

June 30, 1942

Sarah *(his sister)* wrote me that my block is putting up a service flag to include the name & rank of every resident on our block serving Uncle Sam. My name & rank will be included.

July 8, 1942

I was amused at your description of the gas situation --- just enough gas for this and for that. Well, that's hardly a sacrifice with what the soldiers & sailors go through. Everyone must realize that all kinds of sacrifices will win this war for otherwise, we'll all have to sacrifice everything in the end.

We are going to have a big promotion celebration on the post. The newly promoted officers chip in… It will be held in the Officers' Club and will probably be a dinner-dance for all the officers on the post.

We were supposed to run this party before, but it was held up on account of the transfers. Now that our unit is stabilized we decided to go ahead… Most of the officers transferred like it. Many of them have to visit the jungle outposts and do some mighty walking as vehicles or horses cannot, in some instances, be used.

I had to ask one of the…workers for a board. He said "No speak ingles." I spoke to him in Spanish and got what I wanted. So my twenty dollars' worth of Spanish (*lessons*) is quite handy.

July 19, 1942

Last night 16 officers gave a promotion party. I also participated and as a Captain my share was $15. We had a dinner and then a dance. I helped compose some ditties for the entertainment…

We have done fine work with the hospital. It really looks like something. We have converted a lot of waste material into very useful and decent appearing articles.

Beer cans when empty are turned into ash cans, wooden boxes are converted into tables, chairs, serving trays, lamps, etc. I've even had a refreshment stand built for my quarters.

I'm quite used to the noises of the frogs, birds, etc. Although they keep up a constant croaking, etc. now none of us mind it anymore. Even the sandfleas have been tamed.

I'm feeling fine and my head is held high. Our spirits are sky high. We have a job and shall do it.

July 21, 1942

I'm really elated that you are vacationing and surrounded by friends. Somehow soldiers think more of their beloved ones than of themselves and nothing makes me happier than the knowledge that all's well with you and that you are in a suitable environment.

I too wouldn't mind this place so much if you and our "little honey" were present. I too miss you both very much. However, each of us must make a sacrifice. Those in Bataan paid dearly.

We must control our emotions and do what we can. Even though you are blue I know that you are proud and can keep your head high amongst any patriotic group.

Let's give all for America and we'll give Hell to Hitler!!!

July 29, 1942

Again I was delighted to receive snapshots of my little daughter… I read with interest about her devilry, especially running away…

I'm afraid you'll have to be the disciplinarian in our little family. When I return, the baby will be strange towards me and I'll just have to play up to her for quite a while. I therefore, won't be able to chastise her for a long time, at least until she feels towards me like a daughter and that I'm her Daddy, good or bad.

I began to put all the pictures together and mount them in the album. When it's over I'll have her life story. Every now & then I open the album and look at the "beat of my heart" and it acts like a tonic.

Speaking of pictures, I've had 8x10 photos taken of myself... In about 3 weeks you'll be able to hang me and teach Laura that I'm the responsible officer.

Perhaps someday I may get leave. After being here 18 months, one may apply without giving the excuse of an emergency.

August 20, 1942

I was very sorry to learn of the death of your Mother. Your eulogy was very well expressed and presented... Please convey my condolences to the family.

They certainly needed a General Hospital here and I believe our outfit did a fine job in getting established from scratch.

I was able to take a few hours off and take a little trip with some of the officers. It was our first free hours in about 2 weeks.

We saw some very interesting sights and scenes which I can't describe since it would divulge our location. Someday I'll have plenty to talk about.

The soldiers here are raring to go. You'd be pleasantly surprised how our boys are eager to get a crack at our enemies. Even yours truly has become a man who desires action. The soldiers here are well trained and equipped.

From letters some of our medical officers are receiving we learn that doctors are being called left and right. I'm glad I don't have to go through the procedure of closing an office.

Although I miss you and baby, I look forward to the time when our Armies will have made this earth a better place in which to live.

August 21, 1942

I've just received my own 8x10 photos… I hope my daughter will learn to gaze at the picture and say "Da-da". Wherever I'll be, I'll imagine that. A soldier always loves memories, especially the "sweet and tender ones".

August 30, 1942

I have just returned from the movies… Most of the pictures are mediocre, others are excellent. As one of the officers said, "You can't go wrong on an admission price of 15 cents".

That's one of our greatest diversions. The seats and acoustics are excellent. In addition to the movies, the Officers Club holds a buffet supper dance every Sunday. Not many attend these. At most dances the ratio of males to females is so great that one can't dance much.

This place is really a women's paradise… The law of economics reigns supreme here --- all based on supply and demand. That is why the nurses have more date proposals than they can manage.

September 6, 1942

Last night was Maj. Cohen's first wedding anniversary. His wife sent money to Capt. Robin & requested a surprise party. He got it last night and a good time was had by all. For 3 hours we had a grand "bull session" reminiscing, etc. A sign was put up "One year of marriage, 4 months of bliss".

September 11, 1942

A few nights ago we celebrated the 29th wedding anniversary of Mr. & Mrs. Gorin at their spacious home. All the officers & a few soldiers were invited as well as many of their civilian friends.

Rabbi Witkin made a speech in which he lauded this most gracious couple. Then on behalf of the officers plus soldiers he presented them with our gift, a beautiful sterling silver pitcher which cost about $75. We engraved it and also sent flowers.

After a fine buffet supper we had some entertainment. Mrs. Gorin insisted that I stage a "mock marriage". A soldier was dressed as a bride, another as the groom and I was the rabbi. I gave them a good laugh and staged a good show judging from their comments. Other entertainment followed. One must seek far and wide for such a fine couple.

Tonight those of us who can be spared will attend New Year *(Rosh Hashanah)* services in one of the local synagogues. The Army is graciously furnishing transportation. After the services the Gorins will again serve refreshments in their house.

September 24, 1942

Yom Kippur was not an unusual day. At first I thought it would be harder to fast on account of drinking *(no food or liquid for 24 hours),* but actually I believe I had the easiest fast. Fasting is a sort of tradition with me now. I haven't missed one since Bar Mitzvah…

We conducted services the entire day and at night the Jewish Welfare Board gave the boys a dance-buffet supper.

One of the Jewish couples here…invited a group of us (25) to a Simchas Torah dinner which falls on a Sunday.

October 6, 1942

Last Sunday a few of us had a home cooked dinner buffet style at the Freiers who are fine & sincere people. We had gefilte fish, local style, meat wrapped in cabbage, tongue, etc.

It was a swell change from our cooking. I sort of took advantage and filled up.

What a break for us to have families like the Freiers & the Gorins.

Some movie stars are touring here and will give a performance for our troops. If I can jam in, I'll be in the audience.

October 9, 1942

I'm glad you bought a nice bedroom set. Someday we'll complete a full house.

Yes, you should pay Ann (*my Mom and I lived with her sister, brother-in-law and their 2 children during most of the war years.*) a rightful share. Now that you'll have your own room (*they all moved to a larger place*) pay more accordingly. I insist that we pay our due share... Tell that to Ann & Lou. I think you should pay at least $25 rent.

October 17, 1942

There has been quite an improvement in the post. The dust and heavy mud are less and less due to construction. Even the sandfleas annoy us much less. We ordered them to Tokyo.

The civilians here are also subject to gas rationing, 4 gallons per week. When all of us stop being selfish and make sacrifices we shall win this war. Those dam squawkers who belly-ache about inconveniences should be in the Army & then see what it's like. I've lost all sympathy for everything except will it help win the war.

I'm still nibbling away at the salami. Some nights I get hungry and go to town on anything. Food costs me between $45 - $50 monthly.

October 20, 1942

Some of my patients are men over forty --- single & drafted. I guess all single men up to 45 years of age are liable. We in the Army would like to see the 18 – 20 years old drafted.

October 23, 1942

It's becoming more and more difficult to get certain things. There's plenty to eat though and that counts. Our Army here is well equipped and well supplied and very ready.

I often think of our life after this mess will be over. We'll have much to make up for. Perhaps do a little traveling ourselves.

And so another day passes --- still you're "always in my Heart". When we do meet again it'll be the happiest moment in my life.

October 30, 1942

Please bear this in mind. You can't stop me from buying things for my gals.

Why? Well remember mam that you've had very little out of life.

Your courtship days were interrupted *(Dad was in medical school in Austria)*; your wedded life was interfered with; your childbirth period was so trying --- and above all your material attainments were strictly limited.

Now that I have the chance to improve conditions, no one can stop me. Some spend money on drink, etc. I'll lavish same on those dearest to me. If you could only see my expression of contentment when I read your opinion you'd say "more". While my pockets jingle you'll shine.

Would you care for a fancy table cloth? Incidentally, I can get kislov gloves. What is your size and what colors do you prefer? Of course I'll be glad to buy anything for Ann & her household. Is there any perfume you desire? Just name it and if possible it'll be yours.

Just don't worry about me. I'm not denying myself anything. After all I can't use anything but military apparel.

November 2, 1942

Once again I'm O.D. and during a lull in the admissions am writing this letter. So far, I've admitted 5 patients and have collected about $180... Part of the O.D.'s duties is to keep valuables for the patients who get a receipt. In the morning, the O.D. turns the cash, etc. over to the registrar and gets a counter receipt. Once the O.D. takes the money he must issue a receipt and becomes responsible until released by the registrar's signature the following morning.

Army regulations require the O.D. to accept the patients' valuables. Before the tour of O.D. begins the Ward Officer must accept same. Last night the O.D. had to accept $880 from some Sergeant and there is no way of safekeeping any money until the following morning. The O.D. carries it in his pocket. Thus far no harm has resulted.

November 5, 1942

One day last week I had to make a trip to an island. In order to get there we had to cross quite a stretch of water. Since the crafts used in these cases are necessarily small some of the men get seasick when the water gets rough.

While we were on the way we saw the familiar fin of the shark protruding from the water and only about 25 feet away from us. There were plenty of porpoise jumping out of the water, but most of us were on the lookout for the sharks which infest these waters.

When we finally reached our destination the natives rowed out in their native boats which are made from hollows of trees. For 10 cents apiece they took us to shore.

Well, this tiny village is as primitive as one can expect. Very few houses had electricity. The vast majority of the small huts have kerosene lamps and consist of 1 – 2 rooms which harbor many persons.

I saw some of the natives thresh some of the wild rice. The method used was very primitive. It's all done in a big wooden mortar and pestle.

The natives and especially the children walk around barefoot. Very few of them wear shoes. The houses are wooden shacks with thatched roofs. The whole village reminded me of some movie shot of a primitive spot. I really enjoyed the trip and had some interesting experiences which must remain untold now.

November 7, 1942

Yesterday I received a package from Mother which had been mailed Oct. 9th... As usual the salamis were quite moldy and had a rather not too agreeable odor. I gave them the routine treatment of soap & water & refrigeration and cut the ends off; I guess they'll be edible now.

We were quite elated here over the tidings from Egypt. If the Allies smash the Axis African Army, we shall be nearer our Victory.

I was surprised to learn that one of the ex-Wyckoff interns who finished in '39 is down here... I guess with time everyone will meet in the Army.

I enjoyed the final paragraph of your last letter. I realize more than ever the value of love and family. The thought of my "blue heaven" reunion is the fuel that drives me onward and gives me courage to continue.

ver 14, 1942

the Army is doing something about improving the mess. A Captain from ᴗ ᴗm. spoke to the Mess Dept. about the correct way to cook and he certainly knew his stuff. If his suggestions were followed our food would be tastier and more nourishing.

Food and Nutrition Officers should be cooks and since I know nothing about cooking (and frankly don't care to cook), I'm not the one. This job requires a person versed in both nutrition and cooking.

I try to make up our dietary deficiencies by buying fruit, cheese & buttermilk whenever they are available. One cannot buy fresh milk. Some days we get a glass of fresh milk & others reconstructed milk which although identical in nourishment does not taste as well.

November 20, 1942

Amongst the newly arrived draftees is a 43 yr. old with five children. His oldest son was inducted a week before. From the story I gather that this man wasn't much of a provider anyway and liked to drink.

Evidently the draft board in order to meet its quota will take anyone who can walk. Where young men are available this does not occur.

The news is bright now, but let us not lose sight of the plain fact that it'll be a tough fight, perhaps a long one, involving many supreme sacrifices.

It seems that every time we lose a cruiser, carrier, etc., our citizen critics raise a howl. That is obviously overlooking plain facts. The Japs are well equipped and have a bigger Pacific fleet. Just as one can't expect to win a baseball game by a 25 to zero score, so we cannot expect to win or inflict losses on the enemy without casualties to ourselves.

No matter what our faults have been, our Navy has done a good job. If we had more men of the Roosevelt-Hull-Knox & Stimson type & less Hamilton Fishes, Lindbergh, etc. we might have built up a powerful 2 ocean Navy.

November 23, 1942

For the first time since my arrival here I got a 24 hour pass to spend away from the post. Capt. Grenley and I therefore, made arrangements with Rabbi Witkin to spend the time in the interior. The Rabbi conducts Sat. afternoon services in an interior post where 75 Jewish soldiers are stationed.

We met the Rabbi and Catholic Chaplain and then drove up. At various places on the road we saw the black vultures devouring carcasses of a dog and chicken. These birds actually do a most important sanitary job. As soon as they scent a carcass they dispose of it in a short while leaving actually a bare skeleton.

The game laws protect the vultures. Otherwise, the carcasses might lie around for a long time attracting the disease-spreading flies & insects.

We also passed some scattered villages on the way. A few of them have the most primitive houses --- bamboo framework covered on all sides with a special type of leaves. Others have wooden or cement walls and a thatched roof.

I visited a small fishing hamlet. These fisherman hang their fish to dry in the sun and live in thatched huts with a sandy or earthly floor. I spoke a little in their native language.

The post we visited has a swell beach and we took advantage. As I hit the water I thought of you & baby. Here I was swimming on Nov. 21st & 22nd and you bundled up. We then attended the services in the small chapel the Jewish boys fixed and it certainly is a cozy place. It even has the white and blue star on the outside.

I met quite a number of officers. It's really gratifying to see how Army men help each other.

November 25, 1942

I'm glad I have your measurements *(so he could buy her things)*. Frankly, I'm not satisfied with that for I'd much rather prefer to "size you up" in my arms. I do miss you even though I try to be a good soldier.

I often recall some of our quibbling and feel like a heel for acting thus towards you. After all is said and done, I do love you and always will. Often I wonder why I did so and so… I've had a lot of time to contemplate and with this conclusion: arguments we may have, but I promise to do my best to make your future life a most happy one.

Sweetheart, I just can't wait to caress you. Not only have you been so dear to me, but you've also presented me with a "bundle of happiness", our little daughter. As I write this I have her pictures in front of me. I'm even imaging her walking towards my chair, pulling my sleeve, and saying, "daddy up".

Millions of Americans are undergoing the same "type of loneliness" so that their families may live in a better world. Any sacrifice is worth liquidating those fiendish Nazis and Japs. My blood is already boiling and when the time comes I'll have no pangs of conscience.

And so when Victory will be ours, I'll return to you permanently to build our own home, where our children won't have to wonder about daddy --- for he'll be there, not to gaze on you in a frame, but to serve you and family unto eternity.

On Thanksgiving eve I give thanks to the Lord for you and Laura. May he watch over my two loved ones until my return. Until that lucky day, I'll continue being with you in spirit.

November 28, 1942

Our Army saw to it that we were well fed on Thanksgiving Day. We were served the traditional turkey and other delicacies. Everyone was also given a complimentary package of cigarettes and 2 cigars which I believe were the compliments of the U.S.O.

Of course it was a routine workday for us, but the dinner we ate was of holiday caliber. The only trouble with Thanksgiving is that it comes once a year.

The Red Cross is now a fully functioning branch of our hospital and serves as a local social service. They supervise the recreation of the patients and relieve the officers of many personal duties.

November 29, 1942

One advantage in taking care of a baby is that she gives you plenty of news to write about --- and best of all, it's not censorable. You therefore, have quite an advantage over me.

Our little daughter sounds like a spitfire… Does she like to wear the kimono? I'm constantly on the lookout for baby items which are scarce here. I guess kimonos are about the only things obtainable here.

Nothing new to report from our front. I can honestly say that most of these men are getting better medical care than they would have in civilian life. All types of x- rays and laboratory procedures are at their disposal without the worry whether they can afford same. If necessary they even get special nurses. One of our very sick boys got 3 special nurses daily for 8 days. In private life it's about seventeen dollars a day. Sure they deserve same, and much more.

December 3, 1942

At our last service we had quite a crowd present. Many of the soldiers were new here. Rabbi Witkin introduced one of the visiting Protestant Chaplains who addressed us briefly.

The Army Chaplains I've met have really been good men. They extend a helping hand to anyone, regardless of creed. It's not an easy job to be an Army Chaplain --- especially when one is attached to a field outfit. Many of the men have to be mothered and all their troubles attended to.

For the first time in the history of the U.S. Army our government has presented each soldier with a copy of the Bible suited to each man's creed. The book is a pocket edition and contains excerpts from the Bible. There are separate editions for the Protestants, Catholics and Jews. As we entered the services each of us was presented with the "Jewish Holy Scriptures".

Our own soldiers (210th men), in addition to working in the hospital, must undergo an extensive training program to keep fit. By now they have to perform a number of events in a single afternoon, as walk 2 miles in 23 minutes, run 100 yards in 13 seconds and other events.

We are able to go swimming now so that another diversion has appeared. I believe that in the near future we may get tennis and handball courts.

December 14, 1942

You mention about meeting people whose relatives are in the Army and that they pour their hearts out to you. I'd like to remind all that under Hitler we'd all be slaughtered or condemned to a miserable existence, so why all this sentiment?

Sure war is cruel, but it cannot be waged successfully by sentiment. As Gen. Mac Arthur has said, "We shall win or die" and that is the phrase that all must become impregnated with.

If I weren't in the Army now I'd have been ashamed of myself, ashamed to look people in the eye. Sentiment never won a war, but maximum effort will.

I'm glad you are a silent sufferer. I always admired you for keeping your troubles from circulation. Perhaps your actions might act as a tonic to the weaker ones. I wish you'd express my sentiments to them.

December 16, 1942

I just returned from some bowling with Len & 2 other officers. It's an excellent relaxation and a fine diversion for us. Of course I'm new at the game and will need a lot of practice.

Again business is booming with a few interesting cases. We are writing an article on one of our cases.

I guess that ice cream and sour cream will be limited due to the milk shortage. It's more important to have milk than to fill up on the other non-essentials .

December 21, 1942

I finished my 24 hour tour of O.D. duty and am tired and sleepy now. I'm also scheduled to be O.D. on New Year's Day. It really is immaterial here, as one day is just like the other. We're on a full week schedule, no Sundays or holidays.

The Jewish soldiers and officers in our group are voluntarily relieving their gentile brethren-in-arms of holiday duties. The same courtesy was extended us on Rosh Hashanah and Yom Kippur.

Xmas trees are not available to us. The shipping space must be conserved for food, munitions and mail. Some decorations though are available.

Lately we've seen a few good pictures... Here we go to the movies often despite the picture. After all, it's a good way to kill two hours and for only 15 cents. The trouble is that after the show I often begin to feel lonely for my gals. Pictures usually portray & remind one of his beloved ones. In addition, all the caressing on the screen does not satisfy a person hungry for the soothing presence of all his dear ones.

The trouble with most of us and "me-too" is that we become so snug in our comforts and family life that everything is accepted as routine. Only last night I was…feeling weary. I immediately let my thoughts wonder to you. What I wouldn't have given to lie in your soothing embrace, to merely hug you and stroke your hair or to sit next to you on the couch with your head on my shoulder.

"Alas! What fools we mortals be." Now I realize how dear these little affections were, what they really mean to me. Yes, I accepted them like the air I breathe. Now that they are no longer available I recollect and wake up, "a sadder but wiser man".

Xmas 1942

The U.S.O. and Red Cross have distributed the holiday packages to the boys. A very small tree graces the ward. A special holiday meal is being served. Of course special church services are being conducted in the chapel. This is Xmas in our part of the world.

December 31, 1942

I wish you could send some of your cold and I could forward to you some of our heat. By combining both we could be fairly comfortable.

Our Officers' Club is having a dance and late supper tonight, blackout regulations enforced. As to be expected, I have no enthusiasm. If you were with me it would have been a different story --- one of romance, gaiety and joy.

This New Year's Eve is just another evening for most of the men here. I'm not complaining, just reminiscing. We live like royalty compared to the hell of Guadalcanal & New Guinea, etc. areas. Those men would wish for our comforts.

When midnight strikes, I'll just pretend I'm holding you in my arms and kissing you. It seems a long time, doesn't it dear. Yes, I'm almost gone one year.

My New Year's resolution will be to continue loving you. May the Lord grant peace and victory for the United Nations real soon.

Seven

*T*wo years have passed since Dad entered the Army. Now as 1943 begins there is the realization that this War will not be over anytime soon. It will be a long haul, but duty and allegiance to the U.S.A. come before all to my Dad.

1943 would turn out to be a year of many changes for my Father. He would suffer a great loss and know the joy of becoming a Father for the second time --- life and death balancing each other.

During this year he changed military outfits and locations several times. He went from the 210th General Hospital to the 14th Infantry and finally to the 109th Evacuation Hospital where he remained until the war ended. He worked diligently at whatever task was assigned to him and developed a reputation for getting things done.

After almost 17 months his deployment in Panama ended and his unit was shipped back to the U.S.A. He was quite happy to be back on American soil. However, as Dad had *quickly learned, nothing in the Army is permanent except change. As 1943 drew to a close, the Army had other plans for the 109th.*

Captain Milton Cantor, Rose and Laura, 1943

Eight

January 1, 1943

Our New Year celebration was quite simple. First, some of my more intimate friends gathered in my house for a few drinks & songs. I guess we made enough noise to scare the Japs away.

We then marched to the Officers' Club where men outnumbered the women by 10:1--- yes a woman's paradise. Our detachment band played and if you were lucky enough you finished half a dance without someone cutting in a few times.

Yes we were like kids raising some devilry to mask our innermost feelings. At the stroke of midnight I stood frozen, for I then felt your absence most… And thus ended a lonely adventure. I wish to God that next year I'll be able to celebrate with you.

What a guy you picked for a husband, a real wandering Jew. All your friends seem to have theirs at their side and keep them there. When the time comes, I'll have to make it up to you.

You are absolutely correct in your assumptions that I'd prefer to have you stay home and take care of our baby. It's bad enough daddy is away… You just stay home and keep baby & me happy. By buying bonds with whatever you can spare, you'll be helping Uncle Sam.

January 4, 1943

I have been quite busy the past few days. In the first place, I'm working on the article about our recent interesting medical case…hope it'll be accepted by a reputable medical journal.

We (*3 doctors wrote the article)* have finished writing it and I'm now drawing up the completed form for typing. It's a job to get it typed here. After that the article will have to go through medical military channels and then finally to a magazine for consideration.

In addition, I was called this morning before our hospital C.O….and was shown an order from the Surgeon General's office directing our hospital to organize refresher courses (in practical nursing) for our ward men. The Colonel thought that I was the man for the job and was therefore, ordered to organize such a training schedule and carry it out.

It means that I have to start from scratch, draw up a schedule, organize classes, call on other officers and nurses to act as instructors. I'll bet you never dreamt that Dr. Cantor would become a sort of nursing school supervisor. Anything can happen in the Army and a soldier obeys. I'll just roll up my sleeves and be off.

January 6, 1943

Everyone around here is talking about our departure from Ft. Dix just one year ago. How can any of us forget! We were the first general hospital ordered overseas after war was declared.

You know the rest; but you may not know how much I miss you and Laura. Yes, this war has taught me much.

Wars may bring out the barbaristic and beastly tendencies of man, but they also instill in its combatants the appreciation of the esthetic values in life --- the family, the home and the loved ones. In Army language, lives are very expendable in a war. That perhaps is the reason why soldiers realize that their ways might not have been too satisfactory; that the simple beauties of life might not have been appreciated and taken advantage of as much as possible. That is why many soldiers may return wiser men.

According to the bill passed by Congress last month the uniform allowance has been increased from $150 to $250. We will therefore, obtain an additional $100. All in all, my uniforms have amounted to about $250.

I'm still busy finishing the article and working on that training program. The boys tease me by calling me "Dean of the Cantor College" or "the Cantor Nursing School". I retaliate by saying that I'm going to call on them to give lectures and demonstrations to the students --- some fun eh!

January 13, 1943

After I received the radiogram about my Mother, I applied for emergency leave and finally got same. As soon as transportation is available I'll leave for home.

When I reach the U.S.A. I'll wire you. I expect to arrive in Brooklyn within a week or perhaps sooner.

The letters resume in March 1943. Dad's Mother was critically ill.While he was able to be with her during her final weeks, he had to return to Panama before she died.

March 23, 1943

After the preliminary clearing through customs and military intelligence, I just had time to make the train. When I reached my station I phoned and an Army vehicle picked me up and transported me to my new quarters. These I found very spacious, beautifully located, only about a 3 minute walk from my previous residence.

Later in the evening the boys came to give me a warm reception.... The next question was "did I bring any salami?" They couldn't imagine Cantor arriving without it. Although I had no bread they persisted in opening one. I asked them to wait a day or so until I got some, but their desire was so great that I unwrapped the one Izzy gave me and found it quite moldy.... We washed off the mold & the delicacy was soon devoured. The two other salamis are fresher and in better condition.

When I landed here I began to feel very lonely. I seemed to detest every foot of land the train covered. I was like a dejected stranger. I guess everyone returning from leave experiences the same.

I kept thinking of you and Laura. If you two were present it wouldn't have mattered to me. Your absence was felt everywhere, aggravated by the knowledge that this separation will be another long one. At present this house feels empty.

I guess I'll soon again adjust myself to this life, but I'll never feel "right" unless my blue heaven will be there to share it with me. Why! Because I love you. Many thanks for all the sweet memories which are now the treasured souvenirs.

March 27, 1943

I'm finally in the swing of things and working full force. An order has been issued assigning me Ward Officer of Ward G2 & responsible for property therein. We're a little slow now, but one can never tell. We just got a case of amebic dysentery.

Tomorrow evening I'll have the eagerly awaited salami party. I opened the other 2 salamis and they are in good shape.

Once again my love & heart to my blue heaven --- I hope Laura remembers her daddy.

April 3, 1943

Yesterday I received the sad news. Although it produced a pang in my heart, I was indeed consoled some by knowing the truth, at long last.

These past 2 days I have devoted to reminiscing and contemplation --- as probably everyone else would do. I reviewed my life and when the thought of how Mother could best be described permeated my mind, I immediately found the answer in the immortal words of "My Yiddishe Mamma".

Then I said to myself "What had I done to brighten her old age?" Her new world had been confined to Manhattan and Brooklyn with perhaps an occasional trip to the Bronx or the country.

I soon found the answer and it gave me a vast amount of satisfaction in the knowledge that my Army career had afforded her an opportunity to leave the narrow confines and behold new and interesting places.

Remember how she enjoyed the Thousand Islands trip, Madison Barracks & Bordentown; how only last summer she proudly said that her son sent her to the country; how she loved to be with her favorite Laura Ellen. Yes! Nothing can cause these treasured memories to pass into oblivion and the joy and strength they give me are a source of pride, a bulwark against mental torment.

So the "dear old lady" soon went places, feeling perhaps somewhat awkward with her language difficulty, but discovering new interests, new zest and joy. I know how grateful she became and, in her own quaint way, blessed us for these opportunities. Perhaps as she was lying there so helpless her keen mind was reflecting this --- at least I hope so --- for my own intuition informs me that it was probably her "treasured souvenirs". The tears that come to my eyes seem to confirm my cherished hope.

Now that the good Lord has granted her eternal rest I just know that "Somewhere way up there" her sweet face will beam when she'll be relating to neighbors her "Army sojourns".

She may be gone, but in this heart of mine she'll live forever. Perhaps when Judgment Day arrives she'll express these sentiments to me.

April 5, 1943

So far I've managed to assemble ten officers & soldiers for daily services so that Capt. Halpern (his father died), a soldier mourner, and myself can say Kaddish at least once daily. I conduct the late afternoon service and unless the necessary ten men lose interest and stop coming, we'll try to continue saying Kaddish as long as possible.

April 9, 1943

I sent letters to Drs…*(my Mother was pregnant with their second child).* I informed the latter of the situation & said that you'd be hospitalized wherever he may desire… I mentioned that this will probably be a long war, that I may not return for a few years, and that we wouldn't want our daughter to be over 5 yrs. before another one comes along.

Foods are not rationed here, neither are shoes. Coffee and rice are limited to 1 lb. per customer. Despite all this, you eat better than we do.

Our new Officers' Club was opened recently. It is really a fine edifice, spacious and commands an excellent view of the post. Generally, our station is taking new shape and will probably be a beautiful reservation when finished.

We recently ran through an air-raid drill at night. At least you can go to bed during an alert. No such luck with us as we all have our assignments.

Otherwise it's the old story, work, daily Kaddish, movies, bull sessions with the boys, etc.

April 12, 1943

As I write I look up to gaze on my favorite photo of Laura which is adorning my ward desk. How I would have loved to be with you on her second birthday. Today also marks the fifteenth month of our arrival here.

Last night Mr. & Mrs. Kaufman came over to see our movies and afterwards came over our house. They brought all the material for potato pancakes which were prepared in our own kitchen. About 12 of us shared in this delicacy.

Tonight our dramatic club will present three one act plays… It better be good for vegetables & eggs (stale we hope) are being sold at the entrance.

April 15, 1943

Last night we gave a farewell dinner to Rabbi Witkin who will leave soon. About 32 persons, including a few civilians, attended. The table was beautifully set with exotic tropical flowers. After the usual speeches we presented him with a valise… He had been here for about six years and became our "good will ambassador"…

Stanley got a rowboat so on our afternoon off we got into trunks and did some rowing on the nearby waters. We had to be careful of the numerous tree stumps. It was good exercise and we got sun tanned.

We do not pay income taxes for the time spent on foreign service. However, a report must be filed either now or within six months after the war. I expect to file mine within the next few days.

April 22, 1943

Since I'll still be with the 210th General Hospital till May 1st, I'm taking it easy winding up my affairs. They tell me I'll like field medicine and visit interesting jungle country. Besides, I'll be able to see all my old friends of the 210th anytime, as the distance between us will be a very short one.

About 40 people were down to the first Seder at the Gorins… I put those near me in stitches describing Cantor reporting to the 14th Infantry and the exploits of Cantor's Commandos.

The second Seder was a gala affair in a hotel with Rabbi Witkin officiating. Some members of the various other faiths were also present, including the British representative of the Salvation Army & a few Chaplains; Col. Bruton, our Chief of Medicine, also attended.

A Protestant Chaplain invoked the divine blessings. Interfaith good will was stressed by all. Great tribute was paid to Rabbi Witkin who as you know is leaving next week for….

A USO troupe gave us a stage show last night which lasted over an hour. It was pretty good and we got some good laughs.

May 1, 1943

Last night we had a few of my intimates over to give me a little farewell. Of course, I'll still be able to see them daily so it really is not a farewell. However, it terminates my official association with the 210th.

In retrospect, my membership in this outfit was most amiable. I made some intimate & true friends and that's what counts in life. I'm sure we'll have plenty of reunions.

Col. Bruton gave me an efficiency rating of E=excellent for my work on the medical service. There is one higher rating which is superior. However, I believe I fall more in the E class.

May 3, 1943

Well here I am, at a new post, with a new outfit. My official title is Battalion Surgeon to one of the battalions of the 14th Infantry. Both Capt. Paul and I reported to the C.O. of this outfit 2 days ago.

We were then assigned quarters together so that we occupy a 5 room apartment with a modern toilet and shower with hot water. Thus far only the 2 of us share the entire quarters. However, in case of necessity more officers may be moved in.

Of course, the houses are old; nothing as compared to those we formerly occupied. However, we have a good refrigerator, gas range, etc. In other words, we are very comfortable.

A maid does our laundry for $10.50 per person per month. A native man cleans our house, makes our beds, and shines our shoes for $1 per person per week.

Last night our rooms were just full of fleas and other insects. They are attracted to white surfaces so that our beds looked like flea traps. I called our aid station and ordered an insecticide spray bomb. This contraption liberates a vapor or gas which repels & kills insects & mosquitoes. I sprayed the entire apartment and it was 95% effective. These spray bombs are standard issue items now… Tonight my room is livable and almost insect free.

I eat with my battalion mess. The officers have a separate table. It'll cost me about $21 monthly for food. With the 210th it was $33 per month. The Post Exchange serves sandwiches and drinks till 5 p.m. --- also sells fruits, groceries, vegetables, dairy products, etc. Actually this PX is bigger and sells more items than the other one.

Actually, I worked easier than I did in the 210th. The doctors here hold sick call every morning at 7, Sundays at 8. After that we have sanitary inspection of our respective battalion messes. Every 4 - 5th day one of us is the Medical O.D. and if the soldier requires hospitalization we send him via ambulance to the 210th.

About once every 3 months or so our battalions train in the field and we then go with them to practice field medicine. Since I've never had this experience, I'm looking forward to it.

All in all, I'm with a fine outfit with a nice group of field officers.

May 5, 1943

I'm almost a real soldier now; except for living in the barracks, I rough it to a greater extent. My unit is running a jungle fighter school in the heart of the jungle; so when I got the orders to move, I packed only those items I'll need here, put them in my ambulance and joined the convoy at the end of the lineup.

It was pouring when we left, but soon eased after our arrival at this base camp which last year was part of the jungle wilderness with no roads or pavement. Now it's a small camp with some barracks, a PX and a theatre. Outside of this there's real jungle.

The officer's barracks are small and divided into 8x10 compartments with a box serving as a closet. There's no water in our quarters for washing or drinking. Every time we want to wash or use the latrine we walk down 42 stairs…

The wash room has running water and cold showers. The latrine is next to it and is a pit latrine. This means no running water. You sit on an old fashioned toilet box…

It's a lot of fun though and for the next 4-6 weeks I'll probably remain here and learn a lot about field sanitation. The other infantry officers & the Lt. Col. who is the C.O. here are nice to work with.

May 8, 1943

Now about my work in this jungle camp. In addition to being the Medical Officer, I'm the Post Sanitary Officer. I check on the condition of the barrack screens, latrines, wash rooms, barracks, etc. Of course the mess is the important item to watch. I even test the drinking water twice weekly for sufficient chlorination.

After my first inspection, I found much in a deplorable state. You know that sanitation is an obsession with me. Instead of resting on my buttocks and writing letters, I cut the red tape by going directly to the officers commanding the men I needed for the work and got results.

In a short time I had squads of men repair screens, floors, walls, sanitize latrines, install drainage ditches, construct sanitary boxes for bread & cakes sold in the PX and take measures to protect stagnant water from mosquito breeding.

All this would have taken 2-4 weeks through the usual channels. Of course, I could have sat back and taken it easy. This camp however, needed sanitary supervision badly so I just went to work and got results fast.

I'm with a cooperative group of officers and the Lt. Col. in charge is really "one of the boys".

May 11, 1943

My stay in the jungle camp was short-lived, for we suddenly got orders to return to our base station here. So again, I packed and soon rode back with my ambulance to this post.

Don't ask the reason for the change. That's just the way things are done in the Army.

May 14, 1943

This past week has been the most humid I've experienced in all my life. It's most annoying and uncomfortable. After taking a cool shower & using plenty of talcum I still was bathed in perspiration. I'm writing this letter in trunks and I still feel like a wet rag... To make matters worse, I can't use my electric fan on this post as the cycle frequency is different. There are also plenty of insects to pester us.

I'm getting more and more accustomed to my new place. By this time, I know more of the officers, have made more acquaintances, and a reputation for getting things done well.

May 26, 1943

I'm over at the 210 General Hospital now recovering from a partial tonsillectomy. I had a big piece of tonsil either left or grown back since my original tonsillectomy… I therefore, decided to have the excess baggage removed. It was done under local 6 days ago and I'm feeling fine now… I guess I should be out in 2-3 days.

Len wrote his Mother something about me. If you phone her you'll find out. Tell her first that you know I was in the hospital to have a tonsillectomy, and then expect a pleasant surprise.

I believe that the surprise was that Dad would be returning to the continental U.S. There is a Postal Telegraph to my Mom dated June 15 that reads, "ARRIVED CALIFORNIA SAFELY. LETTER FOLLOWS. LOVE MILTON."

1943

Captain Milton Cantor (left) on Bivouac, Camp Carson, Colorado

Captain Cantor, Pike's Peak, Colorado   Laura, 2 years, in WAC outfit Dad sent

Nine

June 15, 1943

After another ocean crossing we have just arrived on <u>American </u>soil. To be exact we reached San Francisco Harbor just a few hours ago and our entire outfit will be quartered for a few days in that vicinity…in a nearby island.

From here we shall proceed by train to another post on good old <u>American</u> soil. Don't worry however, as from now on I'll be in the U.S.; perhaps far from New York, but still in the U.S.

June 22, 1943

Well here I am with my outfit in Camp Carson, Colorado, about 5 miles from the city of Colorado Springs and 90 miles from Denver. The camp is surrounded by the Rocky Mts. and is about 6500 ft. above sea level.

We left in Pullmans for Colorado. Each train had a doctor who was quartered with a Sgt. (medical aid man) in a compartment with a private toilet. We held sick call in the room and slept there also. One of my soldiers developed

Bronchopneumonia and by wiring ahead to an Army hospital an ambulance met us in Denver and evacuated him.

After 55 hours of travel we reached our destination on a cold dawn… As yet there's nothing definite about leaves. I can't promise anything except that I'll do my utmost to get one. Please realize that my last leave may interfere with the new one. There are men and officers here who haven't had a leave in 1 – 3 years.

The housing situation in the nearest town, Colorado Springs, is the same as in other localities near Army installations, i.e., overcrowded.

June 25, 1943

I go to bed with one blanket and use an additional one before long. The early morning hours are cold; the days are hot and dry & fortunately the humidity is very low… Due to the altitude and dryness our lips, nose, and throat become cracked, dry, and parched respectively.

As yet there are only rumors about the fate of our regiment… The post is so big that we must walk a mile or more to the nearest theatre. The station hospital is about 3 miles distance from us. We get very little Army transportation as they are economizing on gas. Some of our vehicles are allowed only 1 gallon per day so we just walk.

Last night we saw a USO show with the Hollywood stars Marjorie Main and Donald Meeks in a skit. After that we had a bite at the Officers' Club where I was able to order some fresh milk, imagine!

June 29, 1943

I tried to phone you from here but found that it may take 1 – 4 hours to get a call through even after 7 p.m. Here it's not as simple as in New York or where I've been. I'd have to wait in the PX for the call & the former closes early.

As a matter of fact, everything here is a hardship. We have very little transportation, the public transportation is crowded and time consuming; the distances on the post are great... Now the laundry is a problem. The quartermaster laundry will not accept our wash for the next week as they can't get enough help.

Fortunately, at least the QM accepted our last week's laundry which for me included 3 weeks of travel wash. The commercial laundries in town charge exorbitant rates and one has to deliver and call for same.

July 1, 1943

Officers who have had leave while overseas, whether ordinary or emergency, will either not get any or have to wait until the first group returns from theirs. I tried hard to get one now, but was refused and was also informed that the earliest possible leave I may get is in Sept. Would you want me to take it then – if I get same – or wait till you give birth. The only trouble with waiting is that with things as they are we might be sent to another overseas zone before many months go by. One can never tell, so please give your opinion on the subject.

I'm kept quite busy with administrative matters. There's a lot of paper work to be done by the medical officers now. I'm O.D. every 4th day and due to the leave of a Med. Officer, I'll be O.D. every 3rd day.

July 5, 1943

I'm glad you & Laura are in Rockaway. It'll be lots cooler there and baby will be able to recuperate much faster. You don't have to worry about her as the chickenpox scales heal well. My pay check will be reduced by $20 monthly from now on since I'll lose the 10% pay for foreign service.

About a week ago a regimental officers' mess was opened. The charge is one dollar per day and so far the meals have been swell. Just one decent meal in town costs over a dollar.

I am still kept busy examining our men. No soldier in our group may go on furlough without a certificate from the medical officer certifying that he is free of venereal diseases. Thus far I've discovered 3 suspicious cases in my battalion.

July 11, 1943

I'm afraid I can't help you much in your problem with Laura. It's pretty tough to raise a child under your circumstances. Perhaps the future will be brighter.

It's your sacrifice for your country --- just like thousands of others. It's probably worse for the "women who wait" than for us, since most of the suspense is with you.

After discovering that the USO in Colorado Springs has a "Kosher Kitchen" a few of us visited it and discovered that it is really a place to go to get salami & pastrami & pumpernickel. Enough said though, we dug in and annihilated some of these tasty morsels… It's only 15 cents for a sandwich, salami costs 10 cents.

This town is quite a contrast to those in my previous location. It is clean and attractive. One is contented to know that a good soda, milk drink or good food can be had in most stores; and one doesn't have to be afraid to consume same.

In addition, there are many scenic attractions. I wrote you about my trip to Pike's Peak… This coming weekend I may go to Denver which is a 2 hour trip. I'm not O.D. so I'll try to see the mile high city with a few other officers.

July 13, 1943

At least during the daytime I'm occupied; but, the evenings and nights are lonely and I long for you and baby. So far my return to the states hasn't been too enthusiastic; I'm just as far from you now as I was before.

I purchased a small frame for the picture of Laura saluting in her wac uniform.

She really looks adorable and I often gaze at her pretty face.

July 16, 1943

I believe I'll get (probably) a 3 weeks' furlough about the middle of August. Of course, this is not very definite, but it'll probably be so; I hope anyways.

Our unit is now being incorporated into the 71st division which is part of the 2nd Army --- until yesterday we belonged to the 3rd Army.

July 21, 1943

As long as I'm with this outfit the chances for promotion will be nil. The Tables of Organization (T.O.) call for only 1 major, the regimental surgeon, and we have one. Perhaps I may get a break and be transferred to an outfit where there's a chance for advancement. There's about a $95 difference in pay between the 2 grades.

July 24, 1943

Yesterday my battalion took a practice hike covering a round trip of 14 miles and a steep uphill climb of a half mile. Most of the way was through rugged country... Our destination was the Will Rogers Memorial Shrine which is 8000 feet above sea level and was completed in 1937 as a tribute to the great humorist...

A few soldiers had difficulty in making this hike. Although I've never done so much walking and uphill climbing before, I did not experience any undue difficulty. Of course, the worst part was the 1/2 mile uphill climb.

I'm kind of getting used to this "mile above sea level environment". The difficulty in breathing and dryness of the mouth and nose has disappeared. I really like this climate and as one officer remarked, "It is good sleeping weather".

Dad got his furlough in late July and returned to Camp Carson 3 weeks later.

August 16, 1943

After a crowded, but uneventful trip I finally reached Camp Carson this morning. About 25 minutes after leaving you my train was already speeding through country landscape and my thoughts also turned "green with envy" at the tranquility of the countryside. Every revolution of the wheel was speeding me towards the military blare.

Upon arrival in Colorado Springs a few of us took a cab & discovered that our outfit had moved to a new area within the camp. At least now we have private rooms and the latrines are in the building so that's quite a break for us. I have my own room which is bare, no closets.

It's getting late and I'm yearning to sleep after 48 hours of travel…

August 19, 1943

Of course our great luxury is in having the washrooms and latrines inside our barracks. Rain or shine we can "rest in peace" and it becomes unnecessary to nurse a "full bladder" thru the night.

Our new location is in a favorable spot. Right in our area we have the PX, tailor, barber, and above all the theatre… We usually go to the 6:30 show; last night I saw "So Proudly We Hail" the movie epic of the nurses on Bataan. Haircuts are 35 cents, movies 15 cents.

Some of the men who've returned with their wives are now having trouble finding dwellings. A 2nd Lt. is paying $21 weekly for a bedroom, private toilet & shower with linens & furniture furnished. His Army rental allowance is $60. Some of the others have been more fortunate paying $55 - $60 for 2 – 3 rooms with a kitchen.

I've learned that my transfer request is now in the Corps Area Headquarters which is a good sign. If it's approved here it'll go to the Adjutant General in

Washington, D.C. which may take another 2 – 3 weeks. So far it's been approved in my regiment & division headquarters.

August 25, 1943

Last Sunday my dental friend and his bride took a few of us to some of the neighboring scenic spots. One was called the "Garden of the Gods" which is really an aggregation of weird & grotesque, huge rock formations.

Yesterday I gave an hour and a half lecture on Malaria, prophylaxis and treatment. About 1 – 2 times weekly each medical officer holds a class for the aid men.

August 28, 1943

Last Wednesday night my battalion left on a three hour cross country march simulating battle conditions. We reached our supposed position in darkness, pitched pup tents & awaited instructions. Then we began the trek back. No lights were permitted so that the problem occurred in total blackout.

During the return trip the word "gas" was passed back and we all immediately donned our masks. I never realized how difficult it is to wear a mask when you're exerting yourself; you must breathe fast and feel as if you simply can't get enough air. It's not hard to walk around with a mask on, but during exertion it's most uncomfortable.

August 30, 1943

I've got some good news for you. I finally got orders transferring me to the 109th Evacuation Hospital which is stationed here at Camp Carson. This is a 400 bed hospital which is sheltered in tents and will have a staff of about 28 doctors.

Evacuation hospitals receive the casualties and the sick from the combat areas. I'll therefore, get a chance to do a lot of professional work when we start operating.

My new outfit was organized last June and at present is training here. We'll probably go along on maneuvers in a few months. I'm most pleased as there's a professional future in this type of work.

My new outfit notified me that I'm also to attend a 3 week course given for medical officers at Edgewood Arsenal, MD., which is about 20 – 30 miles from Baltimore and best of all about four hours from New York. During those 3 weeks I'll be able to make weekend trips to see you & Laura. The course begins Sept. 12th so I'll probably see you in Brooklyn Sat. Sept. 18th. Upon completion of said course I'm to return to Camp Carson. See you soon!

September 2, 1943

By this time I am a full-fledged member of the 109th Evacuation Hospital and have been assigned to the medical service. Of course, at the present time we have no professional work and we function purely as a military training unit. However, once we set up and begin to receive patients we'll be swamped with work.

Most of the inductees we have received are still fresh from civilian life and the system has been changed so that we have to give our soldiers (assigned to our organization) the basic training instead of having them receive same in the Reception Center as was previously done.

Last Monday a 13 week basic military training program was started. Our Plans & Training Officer, a doctor, assigned to me the task of teaching these recruits "Clothing, Equipment, and Shelter Tent Pitching" and so I sat down with one of our 2nd Lts. & a Sgt., worked out a system of teaching & demonstrations out in the field.

Once these men finish their 13 weeks basic training, they'll begin 13 weeks of unit training and after that med. & surgical training. I guess I'll do a lot of teaching once we reach the latter.

Every weekday at 4 p.m. all officers must begin an hour's recreation, or if they went on a hike with the men, are excused… We take the latter in the form of a volleyball game which is usually very spirited.

The chemical warfare course for med. officers will begin on Sept. 12th. I'm allowed 2 days travel time and will therefore, leave here Sept. 10th. Edgewood Arsenal is about 21 miles from Baltimore and about 3 – 4 hours from New York. I'll therefore, see you in Brooklyn the first school weekend, Sept. 18th Sat. and will have to leave again about 24 hours later.

September 5, 1943

I'm very well pleased with my new outfit. Our C.O. is a firm and fair man…

My mess bill now is about 70 cents daily as all our officers eat with the soldiers. We wait about 20 minutes so that all the soldiers have gone thru the chow line, then get our plates & utensils and go thru… We dine at 6:45 a.m., 12:15 p.m. & 5:45 p.m. and have an officers' table. Most of us would rather pay more and have an officers' mess; at present however, we have not enough men to run a mess. The food is good though and here in Colorado there's an abundance of milk, fruit and vegetables
.

Dad took courses at the Chemical Warfare School, Edgewood Arsenel, MD. from September 12 to October 4, 1943. I assume he came to Brooklyn every weekend.

October 8, 1943

Last night we went on a two hour cross country hike and I don't think we missed a hill. It was kind of tiring to climb hills, but we all made it in good shape. At least walking keeps one warm on cold nights.

This morning it was dark & darn cold when I awoke and passing the outside to the latrine did not add to the comfort. I met an Infantry Officer who spent the night in the surrounding mountains. He told me that the water in his canteen froze. The days now are however, so fair and warm that khakis would have been sufficient.

This week I taught sanitation. Next week I'm to teach that plus the treatment of gas casualties. The days are occupied, but the nights are long and lonely and I continue missing you and Laura.

October 12, 1943

The synagogue in Colorado Springs was too small to accommodate the crowd *(for Yom Kippur)*. Anticipating this, arrangements were made with a local church... The facilities of the Unitarian Church were placed at our disposal --- a shining example of interfaith cooperation.

October 21, 1943

This week has been quite a busy one for me. In addition to my usual teaching I had to set up a ward tent, give 2 evening lectures on chemical warfare...prepare an examination in military sanitation which I'm to give the soldiers in two days; and in addition, I'm attending the motor school which is given daily for a week from 1 – 5 p.m.

All our officers take turns in attending these motor classes on the camp grounds. We are taught how to take care of motor vehicles & tires, how to change latter, how to inspect a vehicle, how to clean certain parts under the hood & make minor adjustments & repairs. I guess it'll help me take better care of my own car in the future. This course will also be of great aid in having us take better care of Army vehicles.

Please send me my long (2 piece) woolen underwear... Mail me all the woolen undies you may find amongst my clothing plus any woolen pajamas or woolen socks. I'll need all these for the field work.

Well dearest, loads of luck, love and kisses. I'm sure all will be well. *(My Mother was due to give birth at any time, and in fact, did on this day.)*

October 23, 1943

Yesterday I got the telegram that Lou sent announcing the birth of our second daughter and the good news that you were doing well. I was very happy that you went thru the ordeal satisfactorily.

The cleverly worded telegram also mentioned that you are in the Williamsburg Maternity Hospital so I guess the quarantine at Wyckoff is still in effect. I couldn't leave yesterday to wire you flowers so I'll try to do it today or tomorrow.

Yesterday morning thousands of us were marched to a large field to witness a demonstration in the identification of "friendly aircraft". For 2 hours bombers and pursuit planes flew over us and the identifying characteristics were pointed out to us... It was a very valuable lesson.

Our hospital is now reaching the field stage and we'll spend many hours in field exercises. A few days ago I set up a ward tent consisting of 20 cots. Each such tent is provided with 3 stoves. In one corner is the nurses' office consisting of a box for a desk, chair, and a small medicine cabinet. We use field latrines.

I also have to train our laboratory personnel in the use of the microscope, urine, stool, blood, etc. examinations so that our tent-laboratory will be efficient. Thus far our hospital is considered a fine organization by the 2nd Army Headquarters. Our C.O. is considered an excellent officer and the spirit of our outfit is tops. I'm pleased to be in it.

Well Mother, take good care of yourself and have a well-earned rest. If you desire hire a nurse for a while after leaving the hospital. I'll surely see you in January so until then many thanks for the new bundle (future WAC) and many, many kisses and mucho Amor.

October 27, 1943

The name Sylvia Esther pleases me also… I'm also gratified with the news that you are feeling well and look like new once more. The next time I'll see you we'll do some stepping out. It's about time isn't it?

Tomorrow our entire outfit is going on an all day hike. We'll eat in the field out of our mess kits. We even use field latrines.

October 29, 1943

Our field work is getting more and more strenuous. Yesterday we hiked 12 miles; we had to do a measured mile in 12 minutes and actually performed it in 11 ½ min. During the march an airplane swooped low to give us practice in dodging bullets so I was forced to hug the good earth frequently. My legs feel stiff today, but otherwise I'm fine and have no trouble keeping the pace.

Last night I had to participate in a blackout drive, mostly cross country driving which was very dusty and rough. Once our vehicle hit a hole and all of us went flying to the roof which fortunately was only canvas. Since the windshield is wide open during a blackout drive, it's mighty windy and cold in addition to being bounced around like a ball. When we returned we were glad to consume hot coffee.

Today I taught for 5 hours, setting up a ward tent with 20 cots, chemical warfare, and gas mask drill. I really have been kept quite busy and due to our outdoor exercises sleep like a log.

October 31, 1943

It's Sunday and I'm O.D. --- the day is cold, dreary and raining with some snow flurries. My radio is going full blast and is the only diversion and cheerful note available to me today.

I'm thinking of you, Laura and Sylvia. Laura's remarks to Lou when he slept in our bed "get out of my daddy's bed. I'll tell my daddy, he'll throw you out," amused me so much that I had to laugh every time I reminded myself of same. I guess I have a devout disciple now.

According to Lou's letter you should have returned home *(from the hospital)* yesterday. I'm anxious to hear from you as regards your condition, the birth weight of the baby, etc. Of course you were in no condition to write; Lou's letter lacked much of the desired information and so I hope your letters will furnish it. Did you receive the flowers?

November 5, 1943

Well I'm back from an overnight bivouac and am quite tired… I guess as I'll get more accustomed and hardened it'll become an ordinary routine instead of an ordeal.

Yesterday we hiked 10 miles with field packs, over hills & valleys to our camping area. We had field chow from the mess truck and then pitched tents. I had to give the men instructions in loading and setting up a ward tent; this continued for 2 hours. After that we had more classes & demonstrations.

After supper we made our beds. We slept on cots over which I placed my bedding roll and in which were packed a comforter and 2 blankets. Since we were practicing "combat conditions" complete blackout was enforced. No lights could be shown thru a tent and no smoking after dark. Since our blackout material was poor we just sat in the dark or got into bed. The "gamblers" played cards by the poor illumination of a flashlight… Even though I slept in woolen underwear & woolen pajamas I was awakened a few hours later from the cold & wind…

After a few shivering hours the bugle sounded reveille and all of us had a hell of a time dressing in the cold, washing and shaving in cold water, and above all voiding and defecating in a straddle trench.

How does Laura react to her "little sister"? I guess you'll have to watch the newborn from Laura's "tender care" before she decides to diaper her. Tell my "known dear" that I love her and hope she'll be good to her little sister.

November 10, 1943

Two days ago I received an additional inoculation for typhoid fever. My arm ached for 2 days and yesterday I felt chilly and ached all over. Today however, I felt good enough to play 3 stiff games of volley ball. Three years ago such an injection would "hit me" for about 5 days.

Tomorrow we leave on a 14 mile hike dining on the canned Army rations. We'll bivouac upon reaching our destination and sleep in tents --- if we don't freeze. The morning shave is a job, but orders are orders, so we shave daily in the field.

I've concluded my lectures on the "Treatment of Gas Casualties" and gave a 10 question exam. Now I must mark and grade about 100 papers.

I enjoyed reading your vivid description of our "tiny" daughter. I sort of felt sorry for you, realizing the difficulties you must encounter with our kids.

What a husband you picked out; never around to help raise the family. I wish Uncle Sam could have loaned me out to you to assist in the task, but war is war --- no K.P. for a Capt., eh?

My only assistance at the present is possibly merely to express my love and admiration for you. So Sweetheart, remain fortified in the knowledge that wherever I'll be you will take first place in my heart and thoughts. You've presented me with two treasures which combined with your charm makes me a millionaire.

November 19, 1943

Tomorrow morning is the "big inspection" day. Every nook & crevice of our unit will be inspected, including the officers' quarters. So tonight all of our men are very busy scrubbing & cleaning. They washed all our windows & floors.

Incidentally, since I went overseas there's been a marked reduction in the amount of personal luggage an officer may take on maneuvers or overseas. About 175 lbs. is permissible and this consists of one foot locker, one hand valise, and one bedding roll (in which the blankets & comforters are wrapped).

In addition, our Colonel wants us to limit our luggage to the prescribed amount so as not to overload our trucks on maneuvers… He advised us to send home all our excess luggage.

November 23, 1943

Yesterday the 2nd Army Inspection Team gave our outfit a thorough going-over, quizzing our men in field and medical subjects. They watched us pitch a large tent and set up a complete ward in 33 minutes. There were practical and theoretical questions; such as, shelter tent pitching and first aid treatment for mustard gas on the skin, etc.

Today the Inspection Team gave us a critique and the results. The ratings are unsatisfactory, satisfactory, very satisfactory, and excellent. In order to obtain the latter everything must be perfect. As a whole they graded us very satisfactory --- in some subjects we rated excellent and in others satisfactory or very satisfactory. Our Colonel was well satisfied with the results. Actually satisfactory doesn't mean just passing, it shows that the men performed the task well.

My Chem. Warfare classes & field sanitation were given an excellent rating. The men were complimented on their performance by the examining officer so I'm quite happy over the results.

Starting next week we'll spend 7 days in bivouac and if we get a cold spell, it won't be exactly enjoyable. But that's what is required since we are a field outfit and the field training is important.

We also had the privilege and pleasure of listening to Col. Scott who commanded an Evacuation Hospital in N. Africa and Sicily… His talk was most interesting and enlightening --- and it's no cinch to work in an Evacuation Hospital during combat with perhaps 270 admissions per day of which 200 require surgery.

They kept 4 operating teams going at least on 12 hr. shifts. There were plenty of hardships; you ate C rations (canned foods) for 27 days & took a bath in your helmet liner when possible. You washed your own clothes also when possible. The death rate was remarkably low, only 1.5% in Evacuation Hosp…something the Med. Dept. can be real proud of.

Often they'd get over 200 admissions, treat them and evacuate the patients to the rear within a few hours. The hospital got orders to move ahead and must evacuate all patients to the rear before doing so.

While in Agrigeneto, Sicily, Col. Scott was approached by an Italian civilian who had once lived in Brooklyn and so spoke some English. He told the Colonel that New York, Detroit, & San Francisco had been smashed by bombs. When the Col. asked where he got the information he replied that the German broadcast in Italian had made these modest admissions.

When Col. Scott asked this Italian what he knew about Russia he replied "Oh Russia is licked & quit the war 20 days ago." This incident occurred last summer when the Russians were beating the Germans back all over. It just shows that in propaganda people will believe just what they desire.

It's time to retire for I'm up at 6 so I'll just dream of a family life denied us for the present.

November 25, 1943

We have just finished our Thanksgiving dinner which was also attended by the offices & families and soldiers & their wives. The meal was excellent and I'm just full of good food. We even brought in a stretcher to carry Capt.....who had become immobile from the feast. I thought of just two years ago when you attended our Thanksgiving dinner at Ft. Dix. I recalled Laura trying to sit up in her carriage and look around… That's all I do now is live on memories and future plans.

I hope you'll have a pleasant holiday. We still have lots to be thankful for --- especially for being Americans. I'm most grateful for my three queens whom I love so much.

November 27, 1943

Your last letter seemed to contain misapprehension about my future; especially concerning overseas. I'll try to clarify our status as far as we ourselves are aware of it. You must remember though that in wartime the Army does not and cannot maintain a strict schedule, especially in this changing conflict.

Every officer will get a leave of 7 days plus travel time before maneuvers begin.

My turn will be on Jan. 11 – 24th (7days plus travel time; I must return by midnight of the 24th)…. By the end of Jan. all of our officers, plus enlisted men will have returned from furlough. We expect to go on maneuvers, probably in Tennessee or Louisiana, Feb. & March. After that anything may happen…

December 6, 1943

Saturday I joined my unit in bivouac. When all the wards & living quarters were up the place really looked like "Tent City". In order to reach it our truck had to go down some very steep hills and bumpy terrain. What a beating these Army vehicles must take.

We had a stove in our tents and this helped. It got mighty cold though during the night and from about 4:30 a.m. the cold kept me awake. The straddle trench latrine was rather cold & windy but I did my duty just the same. Many officers & soldiers became constipated in bivouac.

I am back to teaching Treatment of Gas Casualties. We will spend the next 2 ½ months in unit training with emphasis on the professional angle.

December 8, 1943

My leave is now officially listed as commencing Jan. 9th and is for 7 days plus travel time. You'll therefore, see me real soon. I'll wire you when I reach Chicago.

Fortunately, we are being issued some warm clothing which is most necessary for bivouac. Thus far we received fur-lined field jackets, wool sweaters, and warm scarfs. These items certainly come in handy for winter. It seems as if the War Dep't. is beginning to issue field items even to officers. If they didn't we'd be spending much of our salary on clothing. Then after stocking up on winter items, we'd be sent to the tropics or vice versa.

Tomorrow we are going on an all day march. We'll return to the barracks for supper and sleep in camp. The infantry men go into the field, sleep in sleeping bags, no tents or fires, and have to be up at 4 a.m. for a tactical problem. The early morning temperature is freezing and the poor doughboys have to train like this. At least I sleep in a tent which helps some against the biting cold.

December 10, 1943

We awoke yesterday morning to find a 3 inch snowfall and a moderate wind. Since our training must go on despite the weather we slung our field packs and started off. Over our heavy field shoes & leggings we wore overshoes which felt quite heavy and made the marching more difficult. The fur-lined field jackets

& scarfs kept us warm. Under the helmets most of us wore woolen caps which covered our necks & ears.

So we started the long trek over hills and valleys, over snow and ice, our faces whipped by the moderate wind. We made the 13 miles in about 3 ½ hours and most of us were darn tired when it was over. Not only did we contend with the heavy clothing, but the weather increased the necessary physical exertion. I'm glad we didn't have to spend the entire 24 hours in the field.

There are many colds around here. Undoubtedly the outside latrine increases the possibilities of contracting one. Others claim it hardens us, but one sure thing, it is an inconvenience. Well, the poor men in Sicily & Guadalcanal certainly didn't even have a sanitary outside latrine so what's all this belly-aching.

December 15, 1943

Two days ago we started again on an overnight bivouac. The idea is to practice setting up and packing a tent ward, loading and unloading, convoy movement, and setting up a <u>tent hospital.</u> Our men have to work fast and hard to maintain a reputation of being a mobile hospital…

We even have a bath tent. Pipes containing about 6 portable showers are connected by hose to an outside 400 gallon water tank unit which can be heated. There is also a 750 gallon tank mounted on a vehicle and ready to move. A 3 ton disinfector where clothing, mattresses, etc., can be sterilized or deloused is also part of our equipment. This unit can also supply us with hot water.

Our entire outfit was issued winter sleeping bags and believe me, this time I really enjoyed the field slumber. They can be so zipped that only your mouth and nose show, thus keeping your neck, ears, shoulders, and head snug and warm. Even the feet are maintained at a comfortable temperature as the wind cannot get through. Of course, the sleeper has no room to maneuver and one has to squirm in and out of it, but one is kept warm.

December 16, 1943

Yesterday morning our headquarters suddenly got orders to move to the maneuver area in Tennessee. We are to reach our destination by Xmas, set up an Evacuation Hospital and receive patients. All leaves and furloughs were therefore rescinded,

Our Colonel however, promised us leaves during maneuvers so even though I won't be home as originally scheduled, I'll probably see you within a short time afterwards. Sorry, I'm as disappointed as you undoubtedly will be upon reading this, but that's the Army… Only 10 days ago our C.O. told us that he was informed by superiors that we won't be called to maneuvers till March or so… I had made my train reservation to N.Y. and cancelled same…

Since we are only allowed 175 lbs. I had to dispose of much of my luggage. I sent the book box via Amer. Railway Xpress to Sophie… The wardrobe trunk I sent to you…

Please don't get discouraged. I'm only going to Tennessee, about 38 miles from Nashville. I'm positive I'll get leave during maneuvers or between lulls. Besides, I'll only be about 24 hours distance from N.Y… We expect to be there about 4 months.

I'll be near Portland, Tenn., doing medicine after a lapse of 6 months.

I'm practically all packed now. Since the radio weighs over 40 lbs. I can't take it with me. As is I got my money's worth ($8). In a few days I'll ship it to you…

December 20, 1943

I'm about ready to leave with the outfit. Please don't be upset if you don't hear from me for a week or maybe less. For security reasons no letters may be mailed during a troop-train movement.

Most of the officers' wives have left… No families are permitted in the maneuver area and it's impossible to find family quarters in the nearby towns.

December 25, 1943

Well here we are in the "sunny south". Yes'm we left Camp Carson 3 days ago. The entire outfit had Pullman accommodations, 2 soldiers to a lower berth and 1 to an upper. Each car quartered 2 officers who occupied the bedroom…

I also was the train doctor and held sick call for the unit. Every day the train would stop for a ½ hour or so at some town where we'd all go out, exercise the men, and run thru the streets. This kept the soldiers in shape.

We dismounted at Portland, Tennessee at 4 a.m. so that we couldn't go to sleep that night except for short, sitting doses. Trucks then drove us to the hospital area where we were directed to tents and retired. I covered myself with 4 blankets, but it was so cold and windy that I couldn't sleep so I tried to dream of the comforts of a home, wife and children.

After 4 such miserable hours I got some coffee and began to look around for a new and warmer tent. It so happens that we are replacing the 35th Evac. Hosp. who have been on maneuvers since last June and have winterized most of their tents & wards.

The floors & sides (up to a height of 4 ft.) are wooden, the rest is canvas. Each tent has a field stove and when heated keeps the tent fairly warm. The stove-pipes must be cleaned daily otherwise the soot from our soft coal clogs up the outlet & the fire goes out.

Well I struck a conversation with one of the 35th Evac. Officers… He invited me into his tent… They had one vacancy in their warm tent and invited me to move in. This I gladly accepted… We sleep on cots and in our sleeping bags, no sheets or pillows so that the air pillow is mighty handy. I started this letter yesterday, but my fingers were becoming so numb from the cold that I just couldn't finish it and had to jump into my sleeping bag.

We wash in our helmets & drink from our canteens. I'm still able to use the electric shaver as we have special electric field generators which are turned on from 6 – 10 p.m. and 6 – 9 a.m. We also have a field tent shower.

We eat from our mess kits which we ourselves must wash before and after mess. We often eat and work by candlelight especially during the hours when the electric generators are turned off.

Our latrine is a box, accommodating 4 at one sitting, and the entire mess is enclosed in a winterized tent. The latrine tent is not heated.

It rained yesterday and today and the entire area is actually a pool of mud. You just can't go from one tent to another without sinking in 4 – 6 inches and this mud clings. I've honestly never experienced anything like this mud-sea. Fortunately, most of us have overshoes which are just covered with mud. Our floors have also become mud-coated.

We really are roughing it and I for one will appreciate warm weather and civilization. Here we're away from everything… We're fortunate though for the poor Infantry soldier really takes it on the chin --- sleeping in pup tents, rain or shine, warm or freezing weather, exposed to all the elements.

As yet no news about future furloughs. You're no more disappointed than I am, but living now in rather cold tents with the filth & mud is just a small sacrifice compared with what others are making.

December 31, 1943

Now hold your seat for some good news! Late yesterday afternoon I returned from the undertakers at Nashville where we had taken 2 soldiers who were accidentally killed. When I reported to the Colonel he informed me that orders for me to report to the Tropical Medicine School at Walter Reed Hospital, Washington, D.C. were being issued.

The course begins Saturday, Jan. 8th and I'm to leave here two days earlier. All we do the first day is report get organized, and are then released over the weekend. I'll therefore, probably be off Sat. afternoon (Jan. 8th) and will take the earliest train to New York…

I'm as happy as a lark for I'll see you in about 8 days.

Ten

*T*he year started off with the 109th Evacuation Hospital headquartered at Camp Forrest, Tennessee. The winter was cold and mud was everywhere. Dad was lonely, but happy to do his part so that his children could grow up with the blessings of democracy.

In April his unit was shipped to England. Initially they were billeted in private homes. This was a very pleasant and comfortable experience; the calm before the storm.

Before long, however, they were back in the field setting-up a tent hospital. Soon they would be treating many of the D-Day casualties.

Then it was on to France where they were cheered as the American liberators. The Third Army was on the move and Dad's unit followed General Patton's rapidly advancing Army.

It was a very difficult year. France was experiencing the worst autumn weather in 80 years. Not only were the Allies fighting the enemy, but also the weather. Casualties, both American and German POWs, kept pouring in. Dad was often called upon to translate and had many interesting conversations with the prisoners. His letters often mention Nazi atrocities.

The fighting in this sector was extremely tough. Dad had so much compassion and sympathy for our soldiers. He kept telling my Mother that no matter how bad the conditions under which he lived and worked were, the soldiers in the fields and foxholes had it much worse.

Through it all he kept reminding my Mother had proud he was to be here doing his part to help the American soldiers and to ensure a better world for his family. He also wanted her to be proud of her sacrifices.

War changes those who experience it. Dad writes about the difference between existing and living and the importance of home and family. He had several very close friends. These Army buddies, along with letters and salami packages from home, helped them all get through the war.

Eleven

January 3, 1944

By this time you probably know how the Army is --- nothing definite... except a change... About 24 hours after the Colonel had notified me that I was to go to Washington, D.C. he said to me: "Cantor don't count on that too much. All of our soldiers who were supposed to leave for special training schools have had their assignments canceled. I wouldn't be surprised if yours will also be canceled..."

This morning I was officially notified that my assignment to the Tropical Medicine course has again been canceled. Well, I realize what this means to you. I'm also most unhappy about it; especially after the build-up I gave you. However, this is the Army and there's nothing I can do. Why was my trip revoked? The superiors don't give or have to give reasons. I do believe though that I'll get a leave in a month or so, perhaps for 7 – 10 days. That's my only consolation.

January 10, 1944

I'm so busy these days and the environment is so uninviting that you're the only one I've been writing to or have had the desire to write. After a hard day's work you just return to your tent and try to relax.

During the past 15 days about 1100 patients have been admitted to our hospital --- about 75 per day. Since we are a field hospital we often have to work under distressing conditions, as mud, cold, rain or snow, darkness, & lack of sanitary installations like sinks, running water, toilets, etc.

True we have electricity in some of the wards and in my receiving tents. It often however, goes on a blink and I have to examine the incoming patients by flashlight or candlelight in an insufficiently heated tent.

In short, we live in mud, dirt and filth. A bath is a rare luxury. You should see the poor soldiers being admitted; shivering, covered with dirt, mud and filth of maneuvers which are the nearest simile to actual combat. Yes, maneuvers are tough, but they also toughen you. Some of the medical units have been on maneuvers now for six or more months and have had to move to new locations almost every week.

I had my first night off since arriving here so Sat. night a few of us rode 40 miles to Nashville. It was quite cold riding in a small Army truck for 1 1/3 hours. The town was crowded as usual. We waited for a table & finally managed to get a good meal. We then entered a crowded theatre, but had to leave about a half hour before the show ended as the truck had to start back at 11 p.m. Even when we get a night off we must be rushed.

I was told that my leave will start in 2 – 3 weeks. I can depend on that as all are getting a week's furlough.

The "Sunny South" is quite cold & nasty. Tonight our canvas walls & roof are be-ing flapped about by the cold wind. Thank God the mud dried some. This area looks as if tanks plowed thru it. I'm beginning to feel as if mud is just part of our lives.

I got my laundry back today. We sent it to one in Franklin, Kentucky. The clothes look as if they've just been dipped in water. They weren't ironed and worse of all they've been mixed up. Instead of a brand new woolen undershirt, I received an oversized old one.

The training before Pearl Harbor was a picnic compared to now. At Fort Dix we just worked in the hospital and drilled for ½ hour twice per week. Now we drill and march and march.

Dad finally was granted a furlough. A Western Union telegram to my Mother dated January 16, 1944 says, "ARRIVING NEW YORK PENN STATION MONDAY MORNING PHONE YOU FROM WASHINGTON SUNDAY NITE=MILT" Another telegram dated January 27, 1944 says, "ARRIVED IN NASHVILLE ON WAY TO OUTFIT LOVE MILTON"

January 28, 1944

Well, here I am back with my accustomed environment, back to the rough and hardy life… I found a few changes here. The weather during my leave was rather fair with little rain, thus giving the mud a chance to dry. The engineers are building a road so an improvement is on the way.

When you reply address me as follows: 109th Evacuation Hospital, Camp Forrest, Tenn. By that time I'll be out of this mudhole and live in barracks --- what a luxury!

While in Nashville I picked up my electric shaver which cost $3.50 to repair. It is now operating well. That's my only luxury.

True the leave has sort of refreshed me. During the daytime my work keeps me occupied, but the nights are lonely and dark. Our tents have had no electricity for the past two weeks. Our generators went on a blink. We therefore, use candlelight. So during the long nights I just think of you and the kids. Now that we have a little family it would be Heaven to come Home to. Just remember that you're always in my Heart.

January 31, 1944

Yesterday morning a group of ambulances arrived, loaded us in and drove the 110 miles to Camp Forrest… After 5 hours we finally reached our destination. Anything feels good after weeks of cold, dampness, mud, dirt, and the usual field life. Believe it or not, each officer has a small private room heated by a central hot air system, and boy, oh boy! An inside latrine with running water and hot showers… We sleep in beds with mattresses and linen and we eat out of real plates, no messy mess kits. What a life of luxury! It still seems sort of odd walking on firm ground and getting malted and ice cream from the PXs. Sure there are movies nightly for 15 cents.

I'm the persistent dispensary officer, I guess, for the Out-Patient Dep't. is still assigned to myself. I was therefore, busy setting up one and had to make a few trips around the post to assemble some of the necessary items. At least I have a real barracks with many sinks for a dispensary --- no tents.

February 5, 1944

We're all getting into tip-top shape. I have a well-equipped dispensary to work in, but as luck would have it the cold prevents me from operating in comfort. Something is wrong with the hot-air heating system and it took the engineers a few days to find time for us.

This morning the dispensary heating thermometer read 50 degrees. After a few strongly worded phone calls I finally got some action; the necessary repairs were made, and I hope no more will be necessary. Even our barracks haven't been heating too well. Perhaps the 109th was never intended for real warmth and comfort.

Every time I get hungry, usually evenings, I merely slice some of the salami which is hanging in my room and devour same. Our Chaplain is very fond of salami & pumpernickel and also has a supply of these delicacies --- so have many of the other officers. We therefore, often exchange being "feast-host".

Most of the officers have their wives here and are able to stay away from Camp 3 – 4 nights weekly. It seems that single rooms are not difficult to rent. Of course, I'd love to have you with me, but our kids need you more so daddy will bow to the offspring and wait. At present none of us know the score so we just exist from day to day. Believe me Honey without you and the kids it's just an existence.

I therefore, seek relief from the monotony to live in "our world" where we have our own home and roam and play. I often see Laura climbing on my lap while I open her kiddie book and teach her to read and develop her little mind --- perhaps even developing my own by seeking answers to her famous queries "why daddy?'

I often gaze at her picture and say "the most terrible and cruel sadism that has befallen multitudes of others, especially, tots like you, must not happen anymore. Even the evil roots from which such curses have sprung must be burned out of possible existence forever. You kids must have free and unlimited opportunities for development. You must be reared in the blessings of democracy. Men from all creeds and colors have and are making many sacrifices for such ideals. So kiddie, I'm proud to do the same, especially for you and the others. When the new dawn will show the silver lining, I'll return to make all my dreams for you come true.

February 18, 1944

We got quite a group of officers, mostly in the early thirties, and with a few to about 27 months of Army experience. As a whole these new officers, of all creeds, are a friendly group. Frankly I'm much happier now for I'm sure that I'll have quite a few good friends in the future. Besides, these newcomers are not of the "headquarters clique". In addition, with more doctors we'll have more medical discussions.

I'm the unit Medical O.D. today. I hope however, to go tonight to the post Hebrew services. In case medical services are required our dispensary can always reach me on the Chapel phone.

February 21, 1944

A group of us went to the movies to see the Sunday showing of "The Sullivans", the epic story of the 5 brothers who were killed in action when their ship the destroyer "Juneau" went down in the Pacific theatre. We found the film most entertaining and of course a deserving tribute; they will not be forgotten. You'll recall that a recently launched warship was named "The Sullivans".

February 23, 1944

Camp Forrest is a rather dull place and the nearest town is too small to afford any real diversions. Chattanooga and Nashville are about 80 miles away, in opposite directions. We'll be glad to leave this post.

Remember when someone remarked, "Well you ought to get used to this family separation by now". Easy to say for those who've never known this loneliness and misery. There's nothing nearer my heart than to return to you and ours for I love you so and miss you.

March 1, 1944

We're getting a cold spell here after many days of rain --- no snow, just a nasty cold. Our barracks are not too well heated, but it doesn't matter during sleeping hours as I'm well covered and keep warm. I bought a sleeping bag which cost $15… All of the officers are now sleeping in them as we have no sheets or pillow cases…

Yesterday afternoon I went through the infiltration course where live, 30 caliber machine gun bullets fly about 14 inches over your head as you crawl. First we had to crouch in a trench which was filled with about 10 inches of water and mud. As soon as I jumped into it the water overflowed my overshoes and soaked my feet. As soon as the machine gun began to fire we crawled out on our tummies and continued so for 20 yards till we reached a barbed-wire trap. We then rolled over on our backs and crawled through the wire face upwards, making sure that our helmets stayed on. Then we turned over again on our tummy and crawled another 20 yards and then rolled into another trench where we crouched until the firing ceased and were ordered to come out.

Boy were we soaked with mud and wet. The whole purpose is to accustom you to overhead, real firing and to hug the ground when advancing, otherwise you'll get shot.

When it was over I got into the showers with all my clothes on, scrubbed the mud off, and then soaked the fatigue in Rinso… Now that it's over it goes down on your record for the completion of this infiltration course is compulsory.

March 7, 1944

I have quite a few new friends amongst our newer officers. Capt. S. who is an eye specialist from Chicago, and Lt. C., a neurosurgeon from W. VA., and I are quite close and usually go places together. In addition, there are quite a few other nice chaps so all in all, my previous lonesomeness is much diminished. The three of us often exchange pictures of our kids…

We hold now symposiums on medical subjects and often have interesting and heated comments. This entire week I'm devoting four hours to a very technical discussion of the "Treatment of Gas Casualties" before the nurses and doctors.

Recently a talk was given to us about safe-guarding military information. It was stressed that civilians should be very careful of what they say, ask or write in their letters, esp., to soldiers. I merely mention this to emphasize the importance of being judicious in wartime.

March 14, 1944

You'll notice my new address, so henceforth please use it in all your letters. All our letters are censored. I had a most enjoyable trip to this destination. I learned to play cribbage, a lively card game, and that helped to pass the time.

March 16, 1944

I can inform you now that I'll be in to see you soon. Otherwise, there's not much new. It's the usual routine in the daytime and movies at night.

Dad came home on leave the latter part of March. His outfit, the 109th Evacuation Hospital, left for England in April, 1944.

April 4, 1944

Seeing you and the kids was a genuine tonic to me. I shall always treasure those memories.

England, 1944

Captain Milton Cantor

Twelve

1944, ENGLAND

April 14, 1944

We were alerted the morning after I saw you last and shortly afterwards we sailed. After a rather crowded and "interesting" voyage we arrived safely.

I'm somewhere in England. Will write you more as soon as possible. You can reply by V-Mail or the ordinary airmail.

Yesterday I told my roommate…about Laura's birthday so we sang "Happy Birthday Dear Laura". Tell her that daddy sends her all his love on her birthday – and that goes for you too.

April 17, 1944

This is the first chance I've had to elaborate… I'll try to present a fuller account of my experiences.

From our place of departure we had to carry our own val-packs (valise) and heavy they were. The foot lockers and bed rolls had been sent ahead. The Red Cross women served us coffee, doughnuts, and chocolates at the pier…

We entered the ship in the early morning hours and were given cards assigning us to rooms or cabins. This was done strictly according to rank. Seven captains were in my cabin; the bathroom was between 2 cabins so 14 of us used it. We had 3 upper & lower berths and 1 lower --- I slept on an upper. All tables & chairs were removed so we could crowd into the small space, about the size of our bedroom.

Meals were served twice daily, mornings and early evenings. We had one Seder ceremony on board conducted by a Major, M.C., as there was no Jewish Chaplain. The number of Jews on board was large and almost everyone of us attended the Seder which was held a few hours after the regular supper chow. The Jewish Welfare Board provided the wine, matzos and Haggadahs. The wine was rationed to 1 – 2 glasses apiece so we prayed, drank, ate the matzos and called it a day.

Of course, the ship was crowded. We had various boat drills daily and wore the "life jackets" everywhere… There were some USO entertainers going overseas and they put on one show. The lounge however, was so crowded that most of us, me too, couldn't get in. We also had Red Cross representatives on board.

At the station "over here" the Red Cross again gave us coffee, doughnuts, candy, gum and 1 pack of cigarettes apiece. The smokes were compliments of various USA firms & individuals. A local band played for us before the train pulled out.

As the train roared by people everywhere waved at us. We were thrilled the way the kids (adults too) gave us the V sign. The landscape is pretty. The tidiness of the towns & cities surprised us. We passed bombed areas, but much more of England stands than you imagine.

When we reached our destination Army trucks took us to a place where we were fed and instructed. The first night we slept in a large dormitory. The following morning we were billeted.

Every one of us was therefore, quartered in some British home. A few homes took two, most of us are one to a house. I'm billeted in a police sergeant's home in a large room… The bed is dandy and the quilt is warm.

What I say for my landlord, goes for all of them. These Britishers just can't do enough for us. They ask us to make use of the entire house and garden, to bring our friends around, to ask for anything. Yesterday morning (Sunday) I heard a knock on the door. The landlady brought in a cup of tea and asked whether I wanted sugar in it. I knew very well that most of their food is rationed so I replied, "thanks, I drink tea without sugar". She then even offered to make breakfast, but I graciously declined. These people will invite you to dinner and spread their entire week's rations for you. They feel hurt if you decline too much so the idea is to eat a little.

U.S. Army regulations require that none of us may visit town until we've been indoctrinated --- i.e. have received lectures on "getting along with the British". The latter have received similar lectures about us by their own officials… Yesterday we were given the lectures and exam and were then permitted to visit town.

The kids just swamp us with requests "any gum yank, any sweets"? These poor children are really starved for candy, for the ration is very meager. I gave away a few and the smiles on their faces warmed your heart.

I guess 4 of these pages is all that I'm allowed in an airmail envelope…so I'll finish with this request. Please send me a package containing: two midget salamis, some hard candy, some chocolates & cookies. Postal regulations, I believe, require the package not to exceed 5 lbs. & be the size of a shoe box.

April 19, 1944

Last Sunday afternoon we went to town and spent an enjoyable afternoon sightseeing. We entered a restaurant and scanned the limited menu. I guess the days of steaks, meats and chicken are over.

We ordered fish cakes and chips (french fried potatoes)... Butter is just not seen on tables --- fresh vegetables usually are present since every available earth space has been converted to food growing.

The blackout is strictly enforced. We carry flashlights at night. During a fog one can't see for more than 20 inches or so. On a clear night I manage to find my way about without any difficulty.

Of course we use only British money, even in our own PX no American currency is acceptable. The first 2 days we all had trouble with pounds, shillings and pence. After that we began to catch on and by now I'm pretty good at it.

April 20, 1944

Each of us were given a ration card to shop in our PX. We are allowed the following items per week: 7 packages of cigarettes (or 12 cigars or 2 Cows smoking tobacco), 2 chocolate bars, 2 packs gum or roll (hard) candy, 2 boxes matches, 2 razor blades, 1 cake soap. In addition 1 medium sized can juice per month.

We repay the family circle we are billeted with by giving them cigarettes, candy, fruit juice, etc. Since our mess has juice 1 – 2 x weekly our rationed can, can be easily given away without denying ourselves much. I gave the family I'm quartered with 10 packs of cigarettes, chocolate, juice can, the 3 packs of Army K ration I had and a ¼ lb. bar Hershey's chocolate I had from the states. The people were most grateful.

They just can't do enough for me (everyone of us say the same about his landlord). They want me to make myself at home, to ask for anything I need; the Mrs. wants to do my socks, etc. This morning the landlord didn't find me in the bedroom as I was washing so he knocked and brought the tea into the washroom where I was shaving.

They have 2 sons in the Army; one received his air-training in the U.S.A. and informed them of the excellent reception so they're most anxious to recip-rocate. They have an 18 year old daughter...and she told me that in Britain all girls of 18 must register for either munitions work or the Services (Army, Navy, RAF). I believe they ought to do the same back home as too many people are doing useless work.

My present location is quite picturesque. Almost daily we march through the streets and sing.... We have our own mess and rented a room above a pub (tavern) for our Officers' Club. Since we have private billeting we live all over the town. There's also a nice mongrel dog in the house who took to me and I even take him along at times. I get the meat left over from the mess hall for him and the family appreciates it.

Of course, food is strictly rationed all over. The Englishmen don't mind it much because as they say, "it's fair, everyone gets his share". All clothing is strictly rationed. Paper is scarce and rationed...The toilet in the RR station had this sign "due to scarcity ask the attendant for toilet tissue".

There's no central heating. Everyone has numerous fireplaces in his house, one per room. Mine has a fireplace, but since they're only issued one bag of coal per week I don't let them heat it. Bicycles are not rationed and most Englishmen ride them now. A few of our officers bought some. I expect to hire one.

We have a wireless set = radio in our club so we get the news. So you see dearest so far so good. I'm seeing new and interesting people and places, am with many friends and am comfortably situated.

April 21, 1944

I visited Liverpool, the 4th largest city in Great Britain and the second port city. It took quite a bombing and the evidences are everywhere. The docks and warehouses weren't the only ones pasted; plenty of indiscriminate bombing hit some residential sections and a 250 year old church was smashed.

Last night I went to the local cinema and saw "In Which We Serve"… They flash a notice on the screen, "In case of an air-raid the performance will continue. Do not leave unless you reside with a 5 minute walk from here." Of course, there are air- raid shelters nearby. You see them all over.

I do think of you and the kids all the time and I thank God that you live in America.

April 22, 1944

Nothing much new has occurred here except that our training continues. We have, in addition, professional lectures given by our own doctors and each of us is called on from time to time to give a talk on some medical subject.

When the weather is balmy and the sun shines this place is beautiful. Yesterday it rained for most of the day and that kept us indoors. Otherwise, it's training plus outdoor pastimes like rowing, cycling, baseball, volleyball, and bowling on the green.

The English pubs are the social centers of the community. Here they gather to drink and talk. Most of these pubs or taverns have signs No Singing Allowed and also government signs to the effect that minors, under 18 years of age are not permitted in pubs and that it is an offence for adults to buy drinks for minors.

There are no soft drinks or soda fountains. True the pubs have lemon squash with seltzer, but it's not like we're accustomed to.

Paper bags are not to be had. Everything one purchases is carried unwrapped. The British save all salvage materials. They waste very little. They are not permitted to heat their fireplaces in the bedrooms. Electric heaters may be used, but not coal.

April 23, 1944

Last night I went to a Red Cross dance where British hostesses are present to dance with us and keep our morale up. There are younger and older women. A few of the younger ones follow the young soldiers in jitterbug routines.

The American Red Cross took over a large hotel and is therefore, able to offer us many attractions… They even sell Cokes and it's the only place to get one… The band was excellent so we danced till about 10:30 when we had to depart. That's about the only social diversion here to keep going, to keep your mind occupied.

My landlord's twenty year old son was killed at Singapore in 1942. His 2 others are with the RAF and Marines. Tragedy is abundant here.

Today my landlady insisted on serving me breakfast in bed as Sunday we sleep later. Otherwise I'm up at 7 every morning. I didn't want to, but since I give them many items I must make them feel that they are also doing something for me. The U.S. Army pays them about $18 monthly for my room which I think is a good price.

They have a nice garden in the rear of their house and grow their vegetables and fruits. I was told to bring my friends, sit there, and make myself at home. As soon as I get my next week's PX rations, I'll give them some cigarettes and chocolates.

Even though I may be dancing it's you I think and dream about. I'd be in heaven just to be with you and the kids. I often gaze at their pictures and the snapshot of the four of us and dream.

April 25, 1944

Last night we had a unit dance in a local place. The orchestra was good, but the so called coffee was terrible. The British introduced us to a new dance the Holka Polka which is quite amusing and is done by a circle of people. We enjoyed it immensely.

We still haven't had a real warm day. It has rained quite frequently and when it does the feeling is miserable. Then we must crowd into our small club room which is heated by a fireplace and is fairly warm. Since our houses and bedrooms are not heated, it's rather uncomfortable to remain there.

True most of our landlords would heat the rooms for us, but then they'd have to burn their own coal rations so we insist on no fireplaces. I have an electric heater in my room, but I never use it as I don't want to increase their electric bill.

April 27, 1944

I attended a one day school on Medical Installations in the Theatre of Operations. We were given truck transportation to and fro and it was no picnic bouncing around. As we stopped or sped by children continued to ask for these American delicacies *(gum or sweets)*.

April 28, 1944

Our outfit has extra sugar and coal so as a sort of token for the locality's hospitality each of us is permitted to present our landlords with one pound of sugar and 100 pounds of coal. We get it gratis from our unit, place it in containers furnished by the landlords, and bring it to them.

The British sugar ration is ½ lb. per person per week. My billeting family was overjoyed when I brought them the extra sugar. They continue to ask me whether I'm happy with them, to make myself at home, to feel free and happy there.

I'm anxiously awaiting news from you. I realize letters take 1 – 2 weeks, especially air or V mail so I'll just have to wait.

May 2, 1944

The month of real spring has thus far proved chilly, no sunshine to warm your heart. An overcoat is quite comfortable at night and a quilt makes the bed cozier.

The cinema usually presents old pictures so when I find one I had missed, there's something to see. On Sunday evenings the motion pictures are very crowded as there's hardly another place to visit.

Last Sunday evening I had tea in a British home. The host, an elderly gentleman, thought it quite odd that Americans didn't care much for tea. Again I refused sugar as they get a half pound per person per week. I had tea and a piece of cake. These people try to be perfect hosts and offer their own meager rations. We of course, try to be diplomatic. You can't very well refuse, but at least we oblige them by having a little of each.

May 4, 1944

Our unit mail has been trickling in and since morale depends on letters to a great extent, our Colonel has ordered an investigation to find out whether there hasn't been a mix-up in the APO changes.

We march frequently, sing various popular songs while the people stop and stare at us. Many say: hi buddies or there are the Yanks.

Yesterday I listened to a British Naval Officer give us a talk on land mines and booby traps. The British lost heavily when such mines exploded. I believe about 1/3 of all British casualties were caused by such explosions.

Last night some of us again attended a play. We got fair seats for 50 cents. After the show we tried to get tea or a snack.. It was only 9:30 p.m., but not a tea-room or restaurant was open. Even the bars closed a half hour later. Since I'm not keen on the local beer I went home dry.

In my former overseas tour I was able to buy a fair meal frequently. Here one can't do it. At present even our mess is strict with the portions; rarely may we get seconds. When I get hungry I cut a slice of salami and make myself a sandwich. There'll probably be enough left for a week or so. Besides, since I requested some from you and Sophie 2 weeks ago, I should replenish the supply soon.

May 5, 1944

Today was a real holiday for all of us; loads of mail arrived and after many hours of sorting the precious letters and packages were delivered to us. You should have seen the happy countenances of the men and officers. Some got as many as 26 letters.

I understand that there really was a mix-up. Our mail went by error to a different locality. Now that this has been rectified the deliveries will be speeded up.

At present the salami is most welcome. We're getting very small portions of meat and at night we usually are hungry. It seems that the soldiers get enough, but the officers are getting small portions. Of course, I'm only referring to our outfit. I don't know why this is so, but I hope we'll soon get enough meat to satisfy our appetites.

Otherwise things here are about the same. We go to the Red Cross to get showers, coca colas, and a fair meal. Towels and soap are free, haircuts are 16 cents, coca colas are 5 cents, a dinner 25 cents. To dine in a restaurant is too costly. Besides, after 8 p.m. no diners are open.

The soap we buy is unwrapped. Paper is scarce and expensive --- nothing is wrapped. The British are accustomed to it and we are really getting acclimated. Good food and drinks are just memories and no one grumbles about it. We laughed upon reading that fresh eggs are over abundant back home. We don't see any here. Only powered eggs are shipped and what our cooks do to them should be done to Hitler.

May 7, 1944

Your present letter was a testament to your fluency of expression and fine spirits. Though I read it with a lump in my heart I felt proud of your "esprit de corps" and proficiency. After what you've been through these past 40 months – my army duty – you deserve high praise for your courage and stamina. I've reiterated that it's harder on those who must wait, and you, my dearest have had to and still must wait. After victory however, we'll wait together, side by side. So, in your words, "with chin up and smiling face" continue to carry on. I wouldn't want it any other way, no matter what may happen.

May 8, 1944

We're having a unit dance tonight so I'll dance with you in my mind. I'll be thinking of the song, you'll be so nice to come home to. Until then, love and kisses to my gals.

May 13, 1944

I took a trip recently to observe an Evac. Hospital set-up. One of the interesting features was the presence of a kitchen field stove in the receiving tent so that the incoming patients will have hot coffee or cocoa twenty-four hours a day.

From my experiences on maneuvers, I can vouch for the need of hot fluids in addition to the medicines in the receiving tent; especially in cold weather. The equipment, in general, was excellent, most of it being compact and easily transported. Since an Evac. Hospital must keep rolling it must have portable and transportable apparatus.

Last night some of us went to town to a dance sponsored for British Army-Navy Relief. Admission was 65 cents … The couple whose home we visited some time ago asked us to attend and introduced us to a few Britishers. We had a nice time participating in their many group dances like the Holka Polka, Daisy Mae, Valetta and also the Lambeth walk. We dance while we can.

Capt. Folkman and I also visited a synagogue. The Rabbi…greeted us and invited us to homes for the Sabbath eve dinner. They told us that it was their custom to invite soldiers to dinner. We graciously declined since we had messed 2 hours before and knowing their strict rationing, we would have undoubtedly deprived our hosts of their weekly rations.

May 16, 1944

We (*his Army Medical Corps friends*) all have one thing and aim in common and that is to get it over with and return to our loved ones. While we might be having fun it's still of the Laugh Clown Laugh variety – for my heart and mind, as well as theirs, is where mine and theirs are.

So remember that wherever I'll be and whatever happens my heart will belong to you and ours. Always bear this in mind and impress it on my little honey and baby when she'll be able to understand.

May 17, 1944

Your letter postmarked May 9th just arrived. It seems that your airmail takes about a week to reach me. Well, as long as I get them I'm satisfied. I write frequently, at least three times weekly, often more so.

The situation here is about the same. I've been to a few more British homes and have become more acquainted with their aims and aspirations. The Englishman too wants peace and a decent standard of living. Some of them have described to me the bombings. They have to be asked about it before they start talking. I repeat that for almost 5 years of war they've done exceptionally well. While the food is strictly limited and not too varied, no one is starving.

You'll probably read much in the papers and hear much on the radio. Don't forget! Do not work yourself up to a pitch. None of these writers or commentators know anything about the invasion. You'd otherwise be worrying while I might be lazily getting sun tanned. I feel proud to be here and do my bit and I'd want you to feel that your sacrifices are also for a noble cause.

Out of this mess and ashes new structures will arise, sturdier and healthier ones, and, our home will be amongst them.

May 20, 1944

All good things must come to an end, and in the Army it's especially true. So once more we packed and made preparations to leave our fine locality and billets for a new location.

Practically all of us had made many friends and it was a regretful goodbye. Our landlords expressed genuine sorrow for a mutual respect had been manifested; in addition our departure meant a loss of some of our rations which they received as a gift from us – as their tenants.

Please send me another package of salami, hard candy, chocolates and cookies. I'll send some to my former landlord. The latter told me that the dog will miss me. This black mongrel really became attached to me, following me all the time and paying attention to my call and footsteps.

The nurses and officers in the outfit remarked about the dog missing me. I used to make every one of them contribute the leftovers for the dog. When I said goodbye to the family the pup had to be restrained for he tried to follow me.

Well dearest, here I am elsewhere in England. During the trip we ate the K (Army) Ration cold as these trains had no provisions for meals. We finally reached our destination safely and live in a field.

Our hospital is set-up and we are to begin professional work. Everything is under canvas. We live in tents, 4 officers to a tent. I'm with Capt's Carl Baron, Irving Schuman and Chas. Lenhoff and we have lots of fun. Where we are, humor is most necessary.

We wash out of helmets and buckets, eat out of mess kits under the sky and use a field latrine. Our luxury is a sleeping cot on which our sleeping bags are placed. The mornings are still cold and it's a shivering experience to get out of the sleeping bag.

During the night my head and shoulders were cold and the draft kept coming in. Tonight I'll put on a woolen cap and cover the shoulders with a woolen muffler. The days get rather warm. All I may add is that we have to sleep with our ears open. However, all is well and I'm in good shape. All of us are paying more attention to the identification of the various aircraft.

It'll be swell to work professionally. At least here the ground and mud will not be as bad as in the Tennessee maneuvers. I hope we'll be able to make some laundry and dry cleaning arrangements. It's rather difficult to do your wash in small containers and in cold water.

May 22, 1944

Our activities continue out here in the field. Everyone is busy setting up and making the necessary adjustments, including the digging of slit trenches in case of enemy bombing.

Yesterday we worked hard doing the necessary pick and shovel work for ditching the tent --- so that in case of rain the water will run off and not into the tent --- and making the canvas quarters livable.

We'll have to do our own laundry and in addition, there are no dry cleaning facilities. You know how dirty one gets in the field. We all get used to it though from shaving in cold water to shivering in the morning dew which incidentally we find as a thin frost in the early a.m.

Now we have field stoves in our tents and we manage to heat some water for shaving. By working some the tents can be made fairly livable and comfortable. We use the British type latrine in which the excreta drop into a metal bucket. This has been named the "Honey Buckets" and the latrine locality we call "Honey Pot Lane". At least this structure protects it patrons from the rain.

A package a month would be welcomed. In the next one also include some raisins --- the natural ones.... If at times you can include a container of date nut bread, fine. Remember that salami is the mainstay.

May 24, 1944

Your package with the 2 small salamis, postmarked April 28th, arrived yesterday. Both were quite moldy and odorous. I'm letting them air out, then I'll wash them and let the sun do the airing and drying. By and by, I'll inform you as to their taste.

I enjoyed the 4 snapshots of the kids and showed them around. I guess every parent is proud of his; I'm one of the proudest and miss them terribly. I was sorry to hear of your illness and hope all's well by now. You are doing double duty, acting as mother and dad. It's a pity, but during my enforced absence keep the home fires burning though alone.

May 25, 1944

Last evening we attended Hebrew services. A Jewish Chaplain came down to conduct them under canvas. We agreed to have weekly services and whenever the Rabbi can't make it, I'll take charge. My unit has 14 officers, 1 nurse and about 9 soldiers of our faith.

Day by day we continue to construct more gadgets from the scraps of wood lying around here. We try to salvage everything possible and use same for all types of construction.

Our only contact with the outside world is via the daily paper, the Stars & Stripes, published by the U.S. Armed Forces in the European Theatre of Operations. It sells for about 2 cents and is an excellent source of information.

The surrounding countryside here is pretty; so peaceful except for the instruments of war which disturb us at times. There are some quaint villages and old structures in the vicinity. In our spare time we take some walks in the country then return to our tent area where we may play volley ball or work around the tent. It's rather cold now so we've stocked up on wood & coal. As I write it's windy and chilly outside and our stove is emitting a welcomed warmth.

Otherwise, it gets lonesome here. We do an excellent job though in keeping each other company and our spirits up. I have some fine friends here and my tent-mates are swell.

May 27, 1944

Last night I was Med. O.D. and had to sleep in the dispensary. I had 2 blankets over me, but continued to shiver and squirm from the cold. Next time I'll either take my sleeping bag along or use extra blankets.

Today was a beautiful May day; warm enough to wear just a woolen shirt. We took advantage of the sunshine by airing our blankets and sleeping bags.

Last night Carl opened a box of salmon he had received so we had delicious sandwiches. Otherwise, if you're hungry at night you can't do much about it except try to borrow from the boys.

The salami is still drying so I can't give you a report as to its tastiness. The one Carl received doesn't look too healthy. We are drying it and awaiting developments. I'm supposed to be the salami expert and our tent is called – Salami Haven.

Last night I conducted the Friday evening services; since the Hebrew Chaplain can't attend anymore, I'm to do the honors. We had a nice attendance and the Rabbi had even left us a 4 oz. bottle of wine for the Kiddush so after the latter, I sipped about a ½ teaspoon of the precious beverage. I guess my Hebrew education comes in handy as I conduct the services.

May 29, 1944

Today was a sweltering day and the inside of our tents was hot. Some of us rolled up the sides of the tent and that helped considerably. We have no iced drinks here, only water and 2 bottles of Coca Colas per week.

The salamis got a bath today and the mold came off. During the procedure the Colonel said that a rag soaked in vinegar will easily remove the mold. Next time it'll be tried. Now they appear wholesome and after a few more days of drying, it'll be ready for our voracious appetites. Don't send me any freshly prepared salamis as these spoil in transit. Make sure they're dried out, the drier the better.

The nights here, though often exciting, get quite lonely. With no motion pictures, etc. there's plenty of time left for contemplation. My thoughts therefore, often turn homewards to you and ours with whom I know my happiness is assured.

May 30, 1944

We've finally installed sufficient contrivances in our tent to hang up all our clothing and valpacks. We even constructed a table from some scrap lumber. All we need now are some chairs and our home will look a la Park Avenue.

One can expect sudden changes of weather all over England… Arrangements are finally being made for an officers' laundry service. We're all tickled pink. I hope this new service will start soon.

A new hot water system has been installed. Previously, we used to heat the water cans over trenches filled with burning wood. The wind would often blow the smoke right into our eyes as we were washing our mess kits.

Now we have a heating unit operated by a gasoline motor which heats the water by a pipe immersed in the can. We also have such a unit in our area so that hot water for shaving and washing is available.

In addition to the weekly PX items we may purchase, there are also certain articles which can be bought on a waiting list basis. One merely has his name put on the list for cigarette lighters, alarm clocks, fountain pens, wrist watches, hair oil, Kleenex & shampoo (for nurses only), etc.

The longer I'm here and the more I see, the less patience do I have with those in the U.S.A. who still complain about taxes, rationing, etc. As far as we're concerned nothing is too good for the soldier. Even Panama was a haven compared to this place. We're not complaining; we want everyone to feel that we must all back the attack.

May 31, 1944

Last night the salami made its debut. The opening ceremonies were held in the presence of my good friends. After the distribution and consumption of the coveted slices, the unanimous verdict was "delicious". I have to be tight with it otherwise they'll eat me out of leg and limb. Besides, here one can't be too free with food.

I've been quite busy these past few days, arranging, organizing, teaching and receiving cases. Most of us function as teams. I head one of the special teams.

I haven't seen a cinema film since my arrival here. Our vicinity is devoid of any entertainment facilities. Volleyball, baseball and limited swimming are our only diversions. We usually have lots of fun during a volleyball game which is by far our favorite sport.

Most of the Englishmen I've met have asserted that America is way ahead of England in the standards and comforts of living. Here they cling to tradition and precedents too much. Changes are like the process of evolution, i.e. very slow in England.

Most Britishers got their impressions of America from the second or third rate Western films which we were preposterous enough to allow exportation and exhibition to a foreign public. In this way many fancy notions and illusions were created about Uncle Sam

Anyways, England and America have lots of common interests and there's no reason on earth why our present friendship should not be maintained post bellum (war).

June 3, 1944

Those latest four snapshots of Laura were most enjoyable to view … I could have hugged her so. Somehow I miss her terribly. How I'd enjoy playing with her, buying her toys and chasing her. It seems like ages since I last held her in my arms. I guess when I get to know the baby as well, she too will sparkle in my eyes.

Since the war is very real to us here we don't talk too much about it. We face it very often; especially at night

The busier we are the more I like it, for then all our professional work becomes very useful. We've got a pretty good organization and you'd be pleasantly surprised to see some of my innovations in my receiving tent or ward.

Sure it's hard work, long hours and lots of responsibility and organization ability. There's great satisfaction though in knowing that our soldiers are being helped and well cared for. The Medical Dept. in general is very well equipped and organized now.

So another day comes to an end. Soon another night will begin and if the sirens don't disturb my slumber I hope I'll dream of my three best gals, of our own love nest.

June 5, 1944

Laura's prayer for me was most touching and I reiterated it to my chums. I guess she senses how much I love and miss her. Please inform her that daddy too prays that she'll be healthy, a good girl and will listen to mummy.

Life here goes on with no diversions, no Sundays or holidays; every day is the same; the work goes on. I've got everything ready and running smoothly. My receiving ward latrine has also been completed and is ready to function. It should serve as a blessing to the casualties for the next nearest one is 2 blocks away.

Last night I cut the second salami with 7 people participating --- so that it didn't last long. Many men have requested salami from home. Just today one officer came into our tent and offered 40 cents for a salami sandwich. The sign in front of our tent reads: Ye Olde Salami Haven.

It's been rather cold, drizzly and cloudy these past few days. We don't mind such unpropitious weather at night since it keeps the enemy away.

Charlie is still the funny man during a raid. Soon after the sounding of the siren, Charlie jumps into his slit trench under his cot. Since he's so big & fat he must first remove the cot before crawling in. A short period of silence follows. Then from the abyss comes Charlie's serious voice:

Hey Milt, where are you? In bed. Hey Carl, where are you? In bed. Hey Irv, where are you? In bed.

Then what the hell am I doing in this hole? We tell him to keep quiet and stay there, but Charlie insists that it's cold and wants to know what to do next. He has more trouble climbing out of his hole than jumping in. I'm thinking of getting the slit trench concession, to sell refreshments and magazines during the time the trench is occupied.

Aren't we crazy? Sure, but it helps keep us in good spirits and we do laugh a lot, especially, when fat Charlie tells us about his family. Yes, Salami Haven is a laughing tent.

France, 1944

109th Evacuation Hospital, Doncourt, Floods and Mud, Sept.-Oct. 1944

Capt. Cantor on U.S. WW I
Monument (1918), Aisne-Marne
at Chateau-Thierry, Aug. 1944

Capt. Cantor (rt.) in Metz, Dec.1944

From Daddy, Somewhere in France

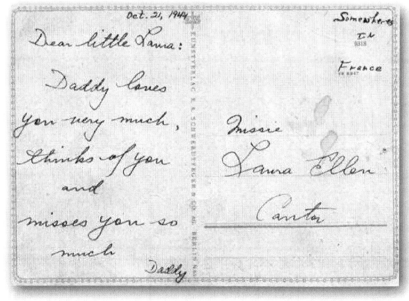

Thirteen

1944, France -- Casualties, Rain, Mud

June 6, 1944

I guess your ears must be glued to the radio, eager for news of our great invasion. Heavy hearts must beat in almost every home in our beloved U.S.A.

Some information I can give you and other I must withhold for security reasons. First I'd like to ask a favor of you and that is please do not worry as I'm fine and in good shape.

True we're all geared up here, working feverishly, making last minute plans and adjustments. Throughout last night we were aware of feverish activity. At about four in the morning some of us were alerted for instant action, the others told to stay in bed and will be called when necessary.

Early in the morning we were given final instructions and we then returned to our wards for checkups and final inspections. Everything was made ready for the reception of casualties and all security measures were taken.

So that's the situation at present and more cannot be said. I'll probably get busier and busier, so if you don't receive frequent letters from me just don't be upset. I might be too busy and not have the chance.

These will be days of action and tremendous responsibilities for all of us. I will carry your love and faith with me wherever I go, wherever I'll be.

June 8, 1944

I was combing my hair outside my tent --- you know, as Laura would say, the few hairs remaining --- when the first ambulance with battle casualties rolled in front of the receiving ward. Everyone was tense as the first four litter cases were carried in.

They consisted of Army & Navy personnel and all were in good spirits. One of the bright spots in the beachhead landings was the absolute Allied air umbrella --- not a single Hun plane was overhead. In some sectors casualties were heavy, in others slight.

There are lots of interesting things I can't write about. Suffice it to say that we here know our latest invasions will succeed. When we ourselves saw the tremendous air support our troops were receiving our hearts were warmed. We even cheered and shouted up at the planes: "Give them hell."

One of the casualties I received was a Capt. who was seriously wounded from shrapnel. One piece hit his steel helmet, made a penny-sized hole, went through his helmet liner, bounced off one of the inner straps in which it made a hole, then went through the helmet liner and stuck between the liner and the steel helmet. His head was not even injured. All his wounds were of the leg. Those helmets are hard to wear cause they feel heavy, but no sensible soldier will part with one, especially when landing on a beachhead.

So we're busy here, working to give medical aid and comfort to our men and Allied soldiers. There's plenty of blood and plasma, thanks to the donors and to the Red Cross. We've been using quite a bit of it since yesterday.

The seriously wounded Capt. received plasma and whole blood and these helped pull him through. Our soldiers have confidence in their Medical Dep't. Everything possible is being done for them.

I'm glad to be part of the big show and we're all glad to do our bit. Perhaps this war will be over sooner than expected and then we can muster all our efforts to crush the Nips. General Montgomery has recently remarked that the Huns will be licked in the not too distant future. He was also most gratified at the excellent cooperation he has been receiving from General Eisenhower's Headquarters.

June 9, 1944

I also received your sweet and tender birthday messages which acted as a tonic during these hectic days. I certainly do appreciate your loyalty and complete devotion.

Here I continue to be occupied with the reception of battle casualties. They come in all sorts of clothing, carrying all types of enemy souvenirs which they insist on keeping. We feel that these American soldiers earned these souvenirs so we check it for them and return it to them on evacuation. The Jerries often wire booby traps to attractive souvenirs so one better beware.

One 2nd Lt. gave us an interesting version of the landings. Those beaches were so crowded that the enemy didn't need marksmen to hit anyone.

I can't tell beforehand when the casualties will roll in. All I know is that ambulances begin to roll in and my crew and I get very busy. No one minds such work because we're helping our soldiers and allies.

June 11, 1944

Yesterday was a busy and active day. Naturally, I cannot talk in numbers. I was however, on the go for 13 hours receiving the wounded. Our paratroopers and airborne troops are pretty tough and had interesting stories to tell. One mentioned that the French civilians were very helpful; 2 of them came running down to our troops and pointed out where 2 Hun machine gun nests were concealed. Our men then made short work of the supermen.

We've also had German prisoners, many of them youths. It seems that the Huns had there either teen men or middle-aged ones.

Our soldiers continue to praise the medical soldiers and officers. Under fire the medicos ran around administering first aid. Many of them made the supreme sacrifice. One of the Chaplains with a Red Cross brassard on his arm fell mortally wounded with six bullets in his body.

June 12, 1944

I had forgotten all about Father's Day until the card from Laura & baby arrived. It made for me a holiday out of an ordinary day. Here every day is the same unless something turns up to pep you up and that sweet remembrance was a good tonic.

Our paratroopers and airborne infantry wounded continue to tell me horror stories of German actions. One said that when his group were forced to leave their wounded they found them dead upon forcing the Germans back and retaking the original positions. A wounded 43 year old Airborne Chaplain said that the Huns fired at battalion aid stations even though the latter displayed the Red Cross emblem.

June 13, 1944

The Red Cross Clubmobile truck visits us frequently and distributes free coffee, doughnuts, etc. to all. In addition every hospital has one of their workers to help the men in all their personal problems.

It seems that the fighting is getting tougher. Our casualties tell me that the Huns are afraid of bayonets and are not good shots with a rifle.

Quite a few French civilians, Fascists & Nazi sympathizers are helping and fighting for the Huns. Of course, the vast majority of Frenchmen are pro-allied and are supporting us in various ways.

June 17, 1944

Now and then about 5 officers at a time may visit some of the nearby towns for a few hours. My turn came and I got into a G.I. vehicle and rode to a nearby town where I saw the sights, saw a picture, my first one in over a month, and then ate in one of the best restaurants in town. I had a fresh strawberry dessert and I hadn't tasted berries in a long time.

Well, it's a good feeling to get away from here and from G.I. chow for a while even though it's only once a month. Just think of those on the Anzio beachhead, stuck there for 67 days.

I took advantage today of the sunshine to air out my sleeping bag and blankets. It's been rather nasty up to now so we're rather enthusiastic about the favorable, sudden change.

For news we are dependent on the radio broadcasts and the ETO (European Theatre Operations) daily the Stars and Stripes. A few of the men have radios so that during our leisure we can listen to the BBC and Allied broadcastings.

June 20, 1944

I'm on the night shift now having changed over with the officer who works with me as a team. If no cases come in I can sleep. My men and I merely stretch our carcasses on litters and blankets and doze off until awakened by an ambulance.

Usually not many cases come in after midnight. I'm on duty now from 7 p.m. – 7 a.m. and will so remain for about 10 days.

Casualties continue to arrive and for military reasons I can't tell you much more. The tales are the same as I've already mentioned. War is hell and there's no two ways about it.

The Red Cross is right on the job distributing towels, shaving equipment, soap, toothbrush, candy, reading material, etc. to our patients and men – all gratis. Most of the patients arrive with hardly anything. As they improve and are able to walk around we even give them a uniform. Our hospital keeps a supply of extras.

And so, as the days pass they bring us nearer to Victory and you and that will be my day of days.

June 22, 1944

Our C.O. promised us that our quota of Majors (6 doctors & 1 dentist) would soon be met. As yet, only the dentist has he recommended; the 6 others are still to be recommended by him to Headquarters.

In point of service, I'm the ranking Captain, but there are many other "political" angles. All I can do is wait; and the Army has given me excellent training in that respect. So I'll keep my fingers crossed and just wait and see. I'm used to having my heart eaten out, nothing ever came easy to me.

Charlie finally received a food package from his wife. It contained a salami which was coated with paraffin and unfortunately this procedure only spoils it. It therefore, had to be thrown out.

Our laundry service has been discontinued so during today's leisure I washed some of my stuff, including scrubbing the leggings. I did a pretty good job even though I hate to do it.

We pay 75 cents per day for our rations and the only other expenses are haircuts, 40 cents and the limited weekly PX rations. I'll probably send you some of my extra money soon. With the $20 increase as foreign service extra pay I get about $96 monthly.

June 23, 1944

Just don't worry about me. I'm in good shape and can function like a horse when necessary. You should have seen my crew and me work during the rush. Our system is really good and quite a few people have remarked about it.

This week I'm on the censoring staff, in addition to my other duties. It's one of those detestable jobs that somebody must do so we take turns censoring the letters of our men and patients. One thing I've learned from reading their mail and that is the tremendous amount of love they possess – half sincere and half baloney. Soldiers are great lovers, but I wish they could express themselves in less words and less mush. I often get a lot of laughs though from this job.

My last letters have not been too interesting. Well you can guess the reason – military security. I can't tell you more, but it's quite interesting and I'm glad I didn't miss the experience.

Today starts my 42nd month in the Army. It's been tough on you, but I'll make it up when I return. It's made me appreciate the value of a home, children and a fine wife, like you.

June 29, 1944

For the past 2 days I was away on a convoy trip to pick up certain supplies. We traveled hundreds of miles through the green English countryside, so peaceful, except when passing through some of the cities where the evidences of the blitz are evident.

I was able to visit my former billeting family and friends I had made in that vicinity where we stopped overnight. We were glad to see each other and chatted much. That night I slept in a real bed and it certainly felt good.

After getting our necessary supplies we started back early the following morning.

The British roads are rather narrow, there are few real modern highways. Many roads are too narrow for 2 Army trucks to travel abreast.

I marveled at our supply and convoy setup in England. It makes you feel good to see the huge amount of supplies available. The Huns might believe that their U- boats are taking a heavy toll of on our ships, but one look here and you know that the Nazis are the biggest liars on earth.

The cooperation amongst various units of our Army is great. All we had to do was drive in at any of our camps and ask for food. At one place we arrived after chow, but they proceeded to prepare a meal for us.

July 1, 1944

I hope our good citizens will never forget how our boys fought and died for all of us *(referring to D-Day)*. I was close enough to see them suffer and I won't forget their faces and exhausted, painful bodies. Yes, the battle isn't over and there's plenty of hard fighting ahead. Have no fear for me, I'll be all right.

Generally, things have quieted down and we have more time now to tidy up a bit. We know we'll lick the tyrants and the consensus average estimate is a few months to next year.

July 4, 1944

Independence Day was just another 24 hours for us. There were no fanfares or celebrations. The war goes on and so do we. The sooner we get it over with the better.

The weather has finally cleared. The sun is really a welcome sight after 7 rainy days. Most of us took advantage of the sunshine to do our laundry. Although

I hate to wash clothes I have no alternative so I just soak and scrub and do a fairly good job. I even scrubbed my field jacket and it's as clean as a whistle.

Tonight a USO show will be presented in our area. I guess we'll have a great turnout. After all, there's no other place to go.

I'd love to eat a dairy meal. What I miss most is fresh milk. Many of the boys feel the same. The G.I. meals are sufficient to satisfy your stomach, but not your tastes or desires. I haven't had a glass of fresh milk since leaving the states. On V-Day I'll try to get drunk on this wholesome beverage. Whenever we get a yellow cheese I always consume it for its calcium content. The Army diet is deficient in calcium, especially in this theater of operations.

July 7, 1944

The Jewish Chaplain phoned me (field telephone) and asked me to spread the word around that services will be held tonight in a Baptist Church which the congregation had so graciously offered us. After the services some refreshments are offered.

Soldiers always think of home and their loved ones. I continue to dream and picture myself playing with the children, walking with them, and above all returning to you, to build and maintain a home for you and ours, a home you certainly deserve, for which you've sacrificed so much and have suffered so. It'll be yours though in the end, to run as you please, to be loved and cherished by me.

July 8, 1944

Confidentially, many of our officers have said to me that if anyone deserves a promotion (to Major) it's I. I refuse to do any catering to the powers that be in our unit. I try to do my work to the best of my ability and not be a mere "yes sir" man. Perhaps eventually I'll get the promotion. I still have my self-respect and the esteem of most of our officers & men, and that to me is more important than bootlicking for a Majority.

A few days ago I lectured to the officers, nurses & men on the Treatment of Gas Casualties. I was complemented on my mastery of the subject by some of the doctors. I'm now preparing for a talk on the Dysentery Diseases which I expect to present before our doctors and nurses in a few days.

July 11, 1944

A few days ago we were permitted to go to the nearest large town and remain overnight. A few of us took advantage of the offer and went. We registered at the Red Cross which maintains sleeping accommodations for us. Another officer and I had a twin bed room with hot & cold water for 80 cents apiece. A civilian hotel would have charged us at least $2.50 apiece.

What a great feeling it was to relax in a warm bathtub and then sleep in a soft bed between clean sheets

I returned to our hospital feeling relaxed and refreshed. Changes are good for the morale, for being in a lonely place sort of gets on one's nerves.

Now it's the same old story, work, march, lecture, eat & sleep. About twice weekly the good old Red Cross comes to the social rescue with movies. As far as all of us are concerned the Red Cross is God's gift to the Army.

July 13, 1944

I was glad to learn that you've finally rented an apartment, your own home. No matter what the expense might be it doesn't matter. In the first place we can afford it, and secondly, it's an absolute necessity which sooner or later we'd have to meet.

I'm sure you'll get accustomed to being at home with just yourself and the children. After all, most women have to and do go through a similar stage. Now especially, with so many husbands away is this true. You're just as solid and have as much fortitude as the other wives and I'm positive you'll carry on.

Get what you need to furnish a comfortable home for yourself and the kids. Just don't worry about the expense, whatever you need purchase and it'll be ok with me. I want you to have a telephone installed which is really a necessity.

July 17, 1944

You know best of all how finicky I am about sanitation. You can therefore, imagine how I dislike sleeping now on merely a cot and blankets which are handed down from one soldier to another. I understand that these blankets are only washed or cleaned about every fortnight.

Well, in the Army one must get used to dirt, sleeping in your clothing, etc. In general the sanitary conditions here are to be condemned, but there's nothing anyone of us can do about it.

The mess halls, barracks, lavatories are all in bad shape. The one cinema is most inadequate and so smelly that we stay away. Besides it's always crowded.

The poor doughboys however, have it much worse. I'm really not complaining, merely stating conditions as they exist.

July 20, 1944

Once again greetings from a new country. I'm now in Normandy, France --- somewhere in the territories we have conquered and liberated. In my next letter I'll write everything --- as far as permissible. Right now I'm tired and am anxious to get this letter off before the mail is collected.

All is well with me, have no fears. I'm glad to be here, helping in the Great Cause.

July 21, 1944

I was about to write you an interesting letter, but we were suddenly informed of new censorship regulations which forbid us to mention our general location.

For the past 2 nights we've slept under the stars. All of us spread our canvases on the ground and covered ourselves with our 2 blankets which I fold double thereby giving me a tent-canvas and one blanket layer to lie on and 3 blanket layers to cover me. I propped my head with that air-pillow. It was warm at first, but got cold about 5 a.m. Fortunately the nights were not rainy ones although cloudy.

Last night we arrived in darkness, grabbed our luggage and went to sleep under the sky. About 2 hours after breakfast (K rations which were heated over a fire we had made) it began to rain and then to pour for about 7 hours. We had no shelter until the tents were pitched 1 hour later. Everything got wet. I repeat though that we were most lucky to have escaped the rain during the night. In such a case all we could have done would be to lie there and get soaked to the skin.

I haven't slept with my clothes off for seven days. I hope to retire tonight like a human being.

Baby is 9 months old today. I do hope I'll be home for her 1st birthday.

July 22, 1944

I am sitting on a cot in a big tent which I share with many other officers. At present we are housed dormitory style in the ward-sized tents; perhaps later we might be quartered four to a pyramidal tent.

The downpour has finally ceased; the cloudiness and dampness persists however, and it is sufficiently cold to warrant the warmth of a fire. As yet we haven't any access to the tent stoves so the more ambitious of us chopped a dead log lying nearby and made an outside fire.

Today for the first time in three days we had our kitchen operating --- 3 hot cooked meals were served us and one can't realize how we welcomed the change of diet. Only one slice of white bread was given per meal as most foods must be strictly rationed for the present.

A huge Red Cross is displayed in our location. Some of our tents also show big Red Crosses. Of course, the blackout is strictly enforced.

Most of us got haircuts from our unit barbers. Our shower tent was also put in operation. We have hot water --- heated by a special field unit heater --- piped to a shower. The water is rationed, but we all managed to get a shower, the first in many days.

Today I round out 3 ½ years of active Army duty. I've covered lots of ground and saw many new places and countries, but the place I care for most and miss most is in Brooklyn, with you and our children, in our own home. I hope our reunion will be soon.

July 29, 1944

Now that the censorship has been lifted I am at full liberty to state that we are in action "somewhere in France". After crossing the English Channel safely, we transferred to an LCT = landing craft tank which then took us to the beachhead won with American blood.

Evidences of battle scars could be seen everywhere. Our men though had performed a miracle in organizing and supplying the landing of our troops. Slit trenches and barbed wires were everywhere; the debris of battle was evident everywhere. During the hard march from the beach to our first destination, we passed through many roads which had signs "mines cleared to sides of road only" or "mines cleared to hedges only". We marched half of the way in complete darkness. Two hours after we had landed enemy planes strafed the beach.

The Normandy countryside is beautiful. The vegetation is abundant and the countryside is green all over. The fields are not too large with hedges all over. No wonder the Huns could hide there or mine them so easily.

The French civilians were really most glad to see and welcome us. Most of the Frenchmen hated the Germans who would take what they wanted, most of the time without paying. The French farmers had to account for everything they used or animals they'd slaughter. As a matter of fact, permission had to be obtained before poultry or cattle could be butchered.

As usual the Americans were free with candy, cigarettes, soap, etc. which we'd often throw at the children or adults as our trucks rode by.

As our outfit later got on trucks it began to pour, but like all soldiers we just took it & got wet. Most of the trucks though had covered tops.

As we rode along the French roads & passed villages and cities we exchanged greetings with the natives. Even small kids gave us the V sign with their fingers. We shouted "Vive la France" & they waved & shouted "Vive La Amerique". The Frenchmen brought out wine & cider and passed it around.

My truck with some nurses in it stopped opposite a house in front of which were 2 elderly French women. We exchanged greetings and then we began to hum the French National anthem "Marseilles". The women were so overcome with emotion that they took flowers from their front garden, made a bouquet and presented it to us. Other civilians actually threw flowers at us; French men tipped their hats and also presented flowers. It was a most touching and sincere welcome.

Some of the villages and towns we covered were full of battle debris. I saw entire buildings and houses blown into rubble. In a three story house I saw the entire insides bare, only the 4 walls remained, yet on the rear wall of the third floor a frying pan was peacefully hanging on it. Frenchmen were salvaging household items. Words aren't sufficient to describe the wreckage.

We camped in a field for a few days. Our Colonel asked us how soon we want to go into action and we replied almost to a man, "the sooner the better". By this time we were anxious to set up and operate. Finally our orders came and we were glad. So again we moved and again passed through scenes I have described.

The few days we were there Frenchwomen came over and did our laundry. They asked to be paid in kind so we paid them off in candies, K rations, clothing, etc. They were sincere, hardworking people.

Within 24 hours we were in action receiving all the battle casualties. We've all worked like hell and are tired. I started this brief 2 days ago, but didn't have the time or was too tired to write.

After working like hell in the daytime, we couldn't sleep at all on account of the many noises, especially the ack-ack fire. It was pretty bad the first 2 nights though now it's quieter. We even watch the tremendous barrage of our ack-ack (anti- aircraft guns) from our tents and it's a beautiful sight, especially when a Hun plane is shot down.

When heavy ack-ack occurs during the time we're in bed we often put on our helmets. So that's part of the picture now.

We're rushed like hell, but to see these casualties come in we feel glad and proud to be here. We also have many German wounded who are our prisoners of war.

I'm usually called to speak to them and interpret. Most of them are glad to be here. All have a great line, stating that they're not Nazis, believe in fair play; especially in their fair treatment.

August 2, 1944

Here it is quite lively and exciting. Casualties and prisoners of war keep pouring in. I'm writing this letter in the dusk sitting on my steel helmet, outside my tent as no lights can be burned in our quarters. It's not comfortable nor relaxing, but it's a luxury compared to our front-line soldiers.

All of us are busy with little time for much else except treating our casualties. You should see how meek and complacent the supermen – Nazis – come in. They'll tell you that they haven't eaten for days, that their wounds are hours old. In the wards they lie side by side to our own American wounded. The walking ones stand in the same chow line with our men.

August 3, 1944

Again I started this letter yesterday evening and was going to finish it this morning before the mail collection, but I got so busy in the Receiving Section and when that slowed down I helped on the wards and assisted … in the operating room all afternoon…

It's a hard grind now, but we like it as that's the work we're supposed to do and help our boys. I see all types of ghastly wounds on our men and the prisoners of war.

The Huns in France know they're licked. Many of them told me that they are forced to fight, otherwise their German officers will shoot them. However, one shouldn't be fooled by their attitude since the Nazis are masters at pleading innocence when they know their cruel game is up.

We got paid in French money. Since we can't buy anything or go anywhere, there's not much to do with the dough. Again I'm sending you a $75 money order. Use it for the house, yourself, kids, or whatever else you might need. Anything remaining can be turned into bonds. I'm glad you received the $100 and $60 money orders. I'm not depriving myself of anything. We've got what we need. Remember we're in fields, not in towns, busy as hell, so what do we need extra money for.

August 5, 1944

Things continue here as previously; we work like blazes for a few days then things calm down and then the storm continues. The wounded continue to pour in and prisoners of war do likewise. The latter state that for the most part they'd like to surrender; especially if they knew they could get such food as we have and a shower and soap.

One German prisoner told me that Hun civilians in Germany are rationed 6 cigarettes per day, soldiers 7 plus 3 they can purchase in the German PX. I showed a Jerry Corporal some of the toilet paper we get in our…rations. He looked and said, "We use such quality paper to roll cigarettes and you use it for toilet tissue".

We have Polish, Russian, Slovenian, etc. healthy prisoners of war working for us.

They claim they are glad to be here and do fine work.

A mobile Quartermaster laundry took nine pieces of our wash and did it for us. They don't iron, but they wash the clothes clean and that helps since we're mighty tired after a day's work to do our own laundry for which we have poor facilities.

August 7, 1944

After caring for many casualties we moved again and on the way passed many bombed places. Dead cattle could be seen in the fields. Foxholes, slit-trenches and dugouts were everywhere.

So once again we traversed through territory over which much blood was shed and bitter struggles were fought. It's easy for armchair generals to predict and discuss, but once you see this difficult hedge grow country you can understand why the battle must be slow and bitter. It's really a miracle how our men were able to advance as rapidly as they did.

Frenchmen on the way again cheered us and gave the V sign. We've cared for some of the native casualties and even treat them in the dispensary.

Somehow as we move forward I feel better for I know then that the nearer we are to our soldiers the better for them. I have little fear. I've gotten accustomed to artillery and airplane bombings and take them as a matter of course.

Yesterday was a red letter day for we received many of the delayed mail. I too was lucky and received quite a few; amongst them were your letters of July 6th and 8th. I had to throw out the second salami... Just remember to wrap all future salamis in plain paper, not wax paper and send me only the hard type... Your package was 6 weeks in transit --- perhaps because I was on the move and the pack kept following me.

Our food now consists of the B ration which means stew meat most of the time. Now and then we may get some pork chops, meat-loaf and butter. Our vegetables vary from this list: potatoes, beans, string beans, green peas, diced carrots, red beets and spinach.

Our PWs (prisoners of war) get the identical rations. I asked the German Sgt. how he liked our food and he replied, "fine". The Polish & Russian PWs who fought or were forced to fight for the Germans said that it was the best food they had eaten since the war had started. The German Army food, according to them, is much inferior to ours.

The PWs are good workers and do everything we order. They seem to be contented here and why not? They are all treated as becomes prisoners of war as stated in the Geneva Convention. The latter permits the use of PWs for non-combat work.

Before they began to work I was instructed to inform them that it is voluntary for them to work for us, otherwise they would be returned to our PW stockade. I explained this to them in German and to a man they stated their desire to work for our hospital rather than to be evacuated to the stockade.

August 10, 1944

After completing one battle phase we closed the hospital, moved to a new locality where we just rested for 24 hours and then got emergency orders to move and hurry the hospital into operation.

So off we went and on the way again passed the usual scenes of havoc. Two towns stand clearly in my mind; the destruction there was devastating.

We were finally taken to our new field location where some cows and calves were grazing and had filled plenty of spots with good fertilizer material. It was getting dark so the hospital wards were set-up in darkness while air and artillery shelling was sounding off only a few miles away and lit the skies for miles around.

No sooner did we have everything in working order when casualties began pouring in and again everyone worked liked hell. My litter bearers are Polish PWs who are glad to work for us and do a fine job in the heavy labor.

After seeing the chaos and destruction of war I'm glad that our people and especially the people of America do not have to experience these horrors. America is a great country, the finest in the world. Let us make ourselves worthy of her.

August 16, 1944

There's a lull now so this morning we were taken by truck to a mobile PX to purchase any necessary items. I bought six pair, all woolen socks and a pair of jump boots, paratroop style. With these you tuck your pants in and don't need to wear leggings.

Together I spent about $8 --- the first money spent in about six weeks, excluding the monthly food bill, 75 cents per day, and for haircuts. They must have a mobile PX which sets up in a large tent. There's absolutely no place to buy anything. The PX prices are very reasonable, only 45 cents for a pair of woolen (100%) socks; in civilian life the boots alone would amount to $12 or more.

I've seen and helped take care of the wounded resulting from mines and booby traps. One of our young soldiers had at least 30 such wounds all over his back & arms & legs. Fortunately, his face escaped. With Penicillin and the Sulfa drugs & Plasma he'll make a good recovery.

August 17, 1944

After reading your description of Smiley (*Sylvia, the baby*) and Laura I took out my small photo-folder and gazed at their snapshot… I always get a lift when I look at them…

The native population continues to come around for dispensary treatment. Many of them have Impetigo --- a nasty skin disease caused by unsanitary conditions. They live in old farm houses and since the invasion have been driven from their homes and forced to live crowded together.

This afternoon a few officers and nurses were taken on a sightseeing tour to a famous monastery. I went along and on the way could see the now accustomed scenes of wholesale devastation.

Overturned, wrecked and burned Nazi tanks and vehicles were everywhere. Large bomb craters, foxholes and dugouts could be seen in many fields. In many open spaces the Nazis drove in many wooden poles to prevent the landing of airborne troops in gliders.

August 23, 1944

We arrived at this new location 3 days ago. To reach it we had to travel over 200 miles. This was done in 2 days with an overnight encampment, since the original location we were supposed to set-up was temporarily retaken by the Germans so we awaited new orders.

The 3rd Army advanced rapidly and we had to follow. Often they'll bypass a town and our armored units will leave it to the infantry to clean up.

As usual, Frenchmen all along the route cheered us, clapped their hands & shouted, "Vive la Amerique." In one city the people hung the American, British and French flags. Some of them gave us tomatoes & pears --- two luxuries for us & we reciprocated with cigarettes, candies, gum & K rations. This particular city had fine shops and showed very little damage.

In a different badly wrecked town we asked the people for bread since many of us were opening canned foods from home. For 2 days we had been consuming the K rations which contains hard biscuits. The trucks would not stop long enough for us to jump off & buy some from the few town bakery shops. Pretty soon bread came flying down to us from windows and we in turn threw back cigarette packs & candies --- fair exchange.

In one of the towns 2 women with their heads shaved were being led through the streets by a crowd of jeering Frenchmen. These two ladies had been consorting with the Nazis and now that the Americans had freed the town, the natives had their sweet revenge. I'm told that the French underground kill all Frenchmen who acted as agents of the Nazis.

Well, we finally arrived at our new location, a large field with plenty of cow flops. Our pyramidal tents, used as living quarters by the officers & nurses, were to arrive the following day with the supply shuttle. We therefore, were given the choice of sleeping outside on the cots and bedding rolls or sleep in a ward tent.

We expected to commence receiving patients the following morning, but we were pressed into service that evening and began to receive patients, so I gave up the idea of sleeping in the ward tent.

I prepared my bed roll & cot… Soon it began to rain & I used all my water-repellant materials & managed fairly well until about 4 a.m. when the rain finally began to seep in and I felt like a baby without diapers. Then to dress out in the rain is another miserable feeling. I usually think of the Infantry, out there at the front in foxholes, and then I grin and bear it.

Frenchmen, old & young flock to our hospital area, for free treatment, for curiosity and to get American food & cigarettes. Women do our laundry, called for & delivered and request payment in food, candies & cigarettes. We supply the soap. I'm told that in town the natives can get 60 cents for a pack of our cigarettes.

So life goes on here. All the sweat & toil & blood of battle winding up here. It's rather ironical when only a few hours ago Americans & Germans were killing each other and then lie side by side in our ambulances and wards.

The Nazis are very complacent and meek when captive. Their attitude is, "I'm just a plain soldier. I was ordered to fight and cannot do anything but obey." They plead innocence and try to reason that Germany needed living space. Many were told & believe that the U.S.A. declared war on Germany.

August 24, 1944

You must have your hands full with the house (*my Mother had moved into her own apartment*) & the kids. Fixing a house of your own certainly requires much work. Aren't I lucky? I always hated moving so just imagine my joy returning to an already established home. As is, I get plenty of moving practice in the Army.

Young and old Frenchmen peddle eggs, tomatoes and other vegetables. It's done on a barter basis as all the civilians prefer food, clothing, cigarettes, etc. to money. It's rather comical to watch the Officers' breakfast line. Many hold the eggs in their hands & hand them over to the cook when their turn comes. It's the old story, "You supply 'em, we fry 'em."

Our hospital has many Nazi wounded and I've had some interesting conversations with them. They are astonished when I tell them that the Nazis declared war on America first. One Nazi Sgt. asked me whether it would be possible for him & his wife to go to Canada after he recovers from his wounds. If he is returned to Germany he believes the Nazis will kill him since as an unteroffizier = non commissioned officer, he permitted himself to be taken captive. A different Nazi however, told me that only those who desert are so punished. I told him that Hitler will be dead by that time.

Just now we admitted three 17 year old Nazis. I examined the papers captured on them and was really surprised at their discipline and blind obedience. They enter the youth units at 10 years and when 14 are transferred into the Hitler Youth. At 16 ½ they serve in the labor battalions and at 17 enter the army so that for 7 years prior to the military service they have already had training in war games and have had their minds poisoned in their supermen & Nazi ideology.

From my many conversations with the Nazi prisoners and the Polish PWs who were forced to fight for the Nazis, I'm convinced more than ever that Germany must be severely beaten and kept down. The poison Hitler has sown in the Huns can only be removed by total destruction; otherwise, we'll be fighting another war in a generation or so.

My Polish PWs hate the Nazis even more than I do. One of them had spent 3 ½ years in a concentration camp and he told me that they'd beat him 3X daily. Of course the food was scarce & atrocious. My Polish PW litter bearers will often jump on a Nazi verbally, especially, when the Huns claim that the Nazis did not commit any atrocities, that the "poor" Germans wanted peace & living room. The Poles point out that the Nazis spilled innocent blood, that they tortured Poles & Jews, etc.

August 29, 1944

We moved again so that by now we're in a different part of France, following our rapidly advancing armies.

A few days ago I went to a captured German medical supply dump which was located in a fair-sized town. I got there somewhat too late as the best instruments & equipment had already been taken by some of the other medical officers and French civilian hospital personnel which was located there. Of course, looting of civilian property is strictly prohibited, but this was captured enemy equipment so we were allowed to help ourselves…

August 30, 1944

Again we've had very little mail for the past 5 days. It's really difficult for the APO to keep up with all the frequent Army movements. Thus far we haven't stayed more than ten days in any one place.

In our last hospital site we were only 30 miles from Paris, but unfortunately, we couldn't get to see it. Thus far we've been near some of the towns which will go down in history as the scenes of great battles. Names like Caen, St. Lo, Mantes, Tessy, Fontainebleau, Etampes & others will remain vivid in my memory.

In one of our locations a soldier came upon a German dugout with a pair of fine field glasses, a very tempting and popular souvenir. We had been warned of how the Nazis mined & bobby-trapped many items which they knew the Americans liked to pick up.

This soldier used his head. First he tied a string to the field glasses and then pulled on them after he moved back about 10 feet. As soon as he pulled on the string & so moved the glasses an explosion occurred which wrecked them, but fortunately left the soldier intact. He still took a chance by playing around with the string…

September 2, 1944

Yesterday we visited the famous World War I battlefield of Chateau Thierry and the scene of the great American offensive which began July 18, 1918 and ended in the German capitulation.

The town itself is in a valley and is a quaint, old city with narrow, winding, cobble-stone streets. The famous Marne River, where so much blood flowed in the first (1914) and second (1918?) battles of the Marne, splits the town in two.

We crossed the Marne on an old wooden bridge and drove to the American (Aisne-Marne) Memorial Monument, a huge structure listing our participating divisions. It is a very imposing American testimonial to her soldiers. The ringing words "Time will not dim the Glory of their Deeds" was inscribed beneath the symbol of a huge eagle.

We then drove….to the Aisne-Marne America Cemetery. Here is the hallowed ground where Americans of all creeds sleep eternally; there is where very tired American soldiers rest after giving up everything to make the World Safe for Democracy.

As we gazed upon the silent rows of granite crosses and the stars of David, we couldn't help but exclaim, "They died in vain". A very imposing Chapel bears on its walls the same details of soldiers who were killed in this vicinity, but whose bodies could not be positively identified. Some of the crosses & stars bore this inscription, "Here in lasting glory rests an American soldier known but to God"; the same inscription as on the Tomb of the Unknown Soldier.

As we passed the towns the Frenchmen, especially the children greeted us & cheered wildly. During one of our stops, 2 truckloads of German prisoners passed and the kids immediately began booing and jeering them. The towns-people cussed the Nazis and told us that the Huns mistreated them.

September 4, 1944

Yesterday I received your package postmarked July 15th. It contained the American cheese, 2 cans shrimp, figs. Everything arrived in good condition. I have now plenty of cheese & other products. I'd like some good salami and a bottle of "Tomato Sauce Cocktail" which is the shrimp sauce. Once in a while include some dried, natural (not bleached or dyed) raisins.

By now you must be in our home. Remember that I'll be there with you. Make it a real home for the children and when I'll return, I'll put on the finishing touches to make it a Home Sweet Home.

September 5, 1944

Today I received your food package, dated July 19th. Although it contained good items like cookies, salmon, sardines & pineapple juice, I was disappointed. I had been expecting some salami, but none arrived in yours, Sophie's or Sarah's packages.

Right now I've got about 4 lbs. of cheese, much canned goods, but no sala-mi. Seriously though, I appreciate the packages whose contents are well chosen. It's time though for some meat; so on with the salami, please. Thanks for the latest packages. I really wanted those cookies.

In yesterday's letter I enclosed a parachute for Laura. The Nazis used it to drop flares. We found loads of them in the woods. I removed the flares & sent the parachute. By tying some weight to the small ring attached to the strings the parachute can be made to work. I guess Laura will have lots of fun with it. I'm enclosing another one…for Ronnie. I sent him a package containing a Nazi canteen & meat can.

We have to ride about 4 miles to our shower tent which was set up near a stream.

There's really a grand feeling when one takes a shower and dons clean clothing.

Today I interviewed some more German prisoners of war; their ages ranged from 19 to 42 years. Some had surrendered voluntarily, others had to be forced. Looking at them makes one mock at the so called supermen. Yet collectively they can be aroused to inhuman crimes & treatment of others.

We found much captured cognac & champagne that the Germans didn't have time to finish so every officer, nurse & soldier received a bottle --- a sort of toast from Adolf to our forthcoming victory.

Thus far I haven't met any Jews in France. The Frenchmen tell me that the Jews were treated badly by the Nazis & forced to wear the yellow Star of David.

September 8, 1944

I received 2 packages from Sophie; both were… almost 6 weeks to reach me. She sent 2 salamis which arrived in good (moldy but that doesn't matter) condition.

Two days ago one of our trucks with 2 officers & 3 soldiers were driving to pick- up our rations. Suddenly they noticed 2 figures step out from the woods, waving a white flag. They were 2 Nazi soldiers, unkempt, exhausted and ragged looking.

They had 2 German revolvers, knife, etc. while our truck being from a medical unit was unarmed. Anyways they were glad to give themselves up with a Sergeant who commanded them.

September 10, 1944

We've just finished another movement to keep pace with the 3rd Army advance. It was a cold, damp, shivering morning. We had a hot breakfast consisting of a canteen cup of hot coffee and the K ration. The ride on the truck was a very windy and cold one. Due to the previous rains and dampness there was, thank God, little dust.

As I mentioned previously the K rations are good, but one tires of them easily. When heating facilities are available the k rations can be warmed and taste swell. The breakfast package contains canned ham & eggs; the dinner *(lunch)* package contains canned American cheese, and the supper package canned pork.

A box of sardines, tuna or salmon tastes much better. Since Charlie, Carl, Irv & I pooled all our packages we have enough. We got some French black bread and had quite a feast.

Again we passed the usual crowds of cheering Frenchmen. The Nazis destroyed some main bridges, but our engineers did some fine work either in repairing or in erecting temporary spans. Those engineers do excellent work and deserve a lot of credit. Often in less than a day they'll construct a bridge across quite a stretch of water.

We passed through famous battlefields, scenes of great struggles in 1914 – 18; history repeats itself.

We were told to expect casualties in a few hours after arrival and sure enough they began coming in. The Huns are trying to halt us and according to some of our soldiers the Nazis are throwing in 14 – 15 year old boys. I don't know how true that is since some might actually be 17 years old, but appear younger.

September 11, 1944

We are covering a very tough sector and in order for our doughboys to get at the Nazis they have to cross a river. The Huns have the entire section well-fortified and from the hill positions command excellent observations of all our movements. Sure we'll get through, but it's a hell for our soldiers.

I wish to God that some of our "griping" citizens could be here and see our wounded and hear their stories. It's difficult to imagine all their sufferings which only a soldier can really understand.

The cold and dampness are causing us much discomfort. The nights and early mornings remind me of Colorado. It's been so cold during the past 2 nights that we squirmed in our beds and went into all contortions to try and keep warm. Then, to dress in the early morning is a shivering experience. We got some stoves into the ward tents, but it is still not too warm.

Just imagine then the poor combat soldiers who have to sleep in just foxholes on these cold nights in addition, of course, to the actual hazards of modern warfare. The days are like real late November days. Remember though my outfit lives like a rich man compared to the front-line soldier.

September 12, 1944

All I can tell you at present is that we are far from Paris, but not too far from Germany proper. Until now we were able to get the BBC war news from London. At this location however, the German stations drown out the English ones so that we can't get truthful versions. We have a short-wave set which might get us the real news.

Our soldiers have captured lots of German warm clothing such as fur-lined vests with sleeves, fur caps and very heavy winter pajamas. Each of us got the latter two while the front line men rightfully received the vests.

Last night I wore my own pajamas and the German ones on top. It helped keep me warm. By tomorrow evening we should have the stoves in our tents.

That new drug Penicillin is used routinely on every wounded soldier and is doing wonders in preventing infections of the wounds. We get an unlimited supply.

September 14, 1944

Again our outfit as a whole received no mail for the past 2 days. The men seem to feel somewhat depressed when that happens for mail call is a great morale builder. It's warmed up some so that the ordeal of getting up in the cold morning is lessened.

Two nights ago Carl, Charlie & I walked over to the nearest village. It was the most primitive & typical French village I've yet seen --- and I've seen many. As a matter of fact, it was typical of pictures of French villages I had seen during the last war.

Ducks were quacking all over; manure piles were evident in many places in the village square. The houses were old with electricity as the only modern convenience. An animal watering place stood in a corner of the unpaved street.

We asked a girl if she had eggs. We were invited into the house which had the stench of a barn. Another woman brought out 6 eggs & we asked for 2 more as our tent has 4 men. When she brought out 2 more we offered to pay but she refused saying, "American, our friends." She then gave us some drinks of wine. We didn't have any candies, K rations, soap, etc. with us, but we'll bring her some.

I was interviewing German prisoners who were supposed to work for us. Amongst them were four Italians who were part of Mussolini's occupation forces in France. When the Duce was overthrown and Badoglio assumed command they were ordered to return to Italy. The Germans however, made them prisoners. The remainder were Huns & to my surprise some were actually 48, 51 & 53 years old. I was told that the 48 – 54 age group is being called up for military service. When the Nazis do that their manpower must be pretty low.

September 16, 1944

The nights have been very dark; in fact so dark that one's vision may not go beyond 3 – 5 feet. Two nights ago I walked out of the receiving tent and tried to make my way to my quarters, a distance of about 2 blocks across the field. To avoid running into 2 tents which had been pitched to accommodate the excess patients I swung left and in the total darkness walked off my course. I walked around for 15 minutes until I could orient myself and find my own tent. Such incidents have happened to many other officers & men.

Ambulances & Army conveys must travel during the darkest nights with just their black-out lights which are dim, tiny lights, barely visible. Well, that's war!

A wounded Nazi was asked to compare the Russian front with the present front in France. He called the Russians uncivilized. When I told him about the German brutalities & their treatment of the Frenchmen…he replied, "I don't believe it." That's typical of the supermen; they either deny their sadism or plead innocence as they were only carrying out orders.

How does a Father explain to his 3 year old daughter why he cannot be with her? Dad tries to answer the question in this letter written to me:

September 17, 1944

My Dearest Laura,

This letter is to you from your daddy. I love you very much and miss you very much. I would like to come home and play with you; take you places with me.

Now I must be far, far away because I am in the Army fighting the bad Germans and Japs. A lot of other daddies had also to go away from their little girls & boys to fight the bad Germans & Japs.

Soon we will win the war and I'll come back to you. I can't come now because we are still fighting.

So when the fight stops I'll come home to you. I'll play with you, bring you toys and take you places with me.

Until then you must be a good girl for Mommy and Daddy and your little sister. If you don't want to get sick you must listen to what Mommy tells you. You want to be healthy and strong for only then can you enjoy yourself. To be healthy & strong you must eat and go to sleep early.

So please be a good girl for Daddy until I come home. When I come home we'll have a lot of fun and good times.

All my love and kisses to you, Mommy and your little baby sister.

Daddy

September 18, 1944

I know it's Rosh Hashanah because our Baptist Chaplain … told me so. The Jewish Chaplain … is conducting services for those of us who can come to a certain town for a few hours. Our unit Chaplain has arranged for transportation.

Somehow our driver lost his way and at a certain fork in the road directed us to a side road since about 2 miles up the main road we were on was being shelled. So we travelled a few miles on this side road until we reached a huge viaduct-railroad bridge which had been hit by our bombers and put out of commission. It was a fine job, a gruesome sight!

We found a sign at this point and it indicated that we had overshot our destination by about 15 miles. By the time we returned to the place where we should have made a left turn instead of a right, it was too late for the services so we ordered the driver to return to the hospital. This ended our New Year adventure.

We've had much rain lately. The ground around the hospital is very muddy & slippery… Inside our wards we have electric lights, but our blackout precautions on the outside are strict.

The field stoves in our tents help relieve the chilliness & dampness. Our men at the front though have no such comforts. They are brought in exhausted; some can't even stand on their feet from sheer exhaustion. Some haven't removed their shoes for 2 - 3 weeks, some haven't had a hot meal for a few days. The Army tries to get the kitchen truck to the men up front, but often this is not possible so our men eat the K or C rations. This sector is a tough one, the toughest we've had thus far.

September 21, 1944

I'm writing this letter in the early morning after a rather busy night. One really can't appreciate soldiers unless one sees them in actual action or the way they appear when wounded.

When the people back home read the newspapers or listen to the radio, they only see the rainbow. Back here we see the storm that finally led to the blue skies and too often it's a terrific force.

I was talking last night to a wounded German Sgt. who lived in Czechoslovakia. He told me that our bombings of Germany destroyed its armament industry &

supplies.... I overheard a German PW litter-bearer say to the wounded German Sgt. when he mentioned about the scarcity of food for the Nazi soldiers, "Here you'll be eating better than you did in peace time."

September 23, 1944

Out this way it's the same story centered about the reception of casualties day and night. We try to cheer them by distributing coffee and unlimited amounts of cigarettes, gum, chocolate & hard candy. The Red Cross representative usually is around to assist in the distribution.

Remember my writing you about the Polish soldiers who were forced to serve in the German Army. As PWs they were working for us. They liked it so much here (even though carrying litters is heavy work) that when the Army recalled them to the PW stockade until a technicality could be straightened out they were heartbroken. After a 3 day absence they were returned to us. You should have seen their smiles. Those who work for my section returned & greeted me with salutes, some with handshakes, and mentioned how glad they were to return to us.

Sometimes I wonder what it'll be like to walk nights in well-lit streets; to read in bed, sleep in a comfortable bed, use a modern toilet & bath and eat real good food. You'll probably have your hands full recivilizing your husband.

I get lonesome upon retiring so I'll continue looking forward to you to improve the situation in a most loving fashion for I love you dearly.

September 24, 1944

Outside the tents the mud is about 4 inches deep; not as bad as we had experienced in the Tennessee maneuvers, but plenty slippery. My zipper-type boots come in quite handy and is the cause of many remarks & wisecracks. Those whom the boots might fit want to buy them from me. Thus far I've had more such offers than hair on my head.

Last evening we were sent a Nazi PW from our prison stockade; he was a member of the SS or storm troops. The tent- ward he was to be admitted to had 2 Free French soldiers, the so-called FFI or French Forces of the Interior. These Frenchmen are not too well disposed towards the Nazis therefore, we had to place superman in a different ward.

The FFI are rightly bitter towards the Nazis for when the latter captured them they'd torture & kill them. You might have read the recent massacre of the town of Oradour in Central France. There are 2 towns with such a first name, but with different second names.

After killing off most of the town's males & burning the houses to the ground, the Nazis realized they had made a mistake for the punishment was intended for the other town by that first name. The Heinies have plenty to be held against them, especially the Nazi party, Gestapo & SS men.

September 28, 1944

Our hospital got so bogged down in mud that the engineers finally had to come in, scrape away the mud with a bulldozer and prepared a firm road. Now at least an ambulance can back up without bogging down.

Yesterday being Yom Kippur we had services which I conducted and which was attended also by our Protestant Chaplain, a Baptist. We held it in his tent. After Yizkor I asked him to say a few words.

Throughout France the Nazis had desecrated the Synagogues and most of the Jews were "shipped away;" I guess either killed off or sent to Poland to work & slave.

Last night we were shown an excellent film called "Gaslight". Most of the time we were shown inferior films, but every now & then a 4 star appears.

October 1, 1944

At times we engage in sentimental conversations. This time we were discussing how little most of us had appreciated the little comforts at home. We had just accepted them as a routine without any thought as to their value. Now however, when they are not to be had or found we finally realize that those little things that go to make a home are more than mere routine. They are the difference between living and existing.

The average soldier in combat merely exists from day to day, becomes more and more aware that his home, wife & children are the sparkles in his life. He becomes remorseful because then he failed to credit his homemakers with their due share.

He resolves now that his present existence must be for the sake of living; living for those days when he can return to his woman, take her in his arms and say:

"I used to take you for granted. As a matter of fact, I thought your services & efforts were due me. It makes war with its brutalities, sufferings and inconveniences to prove to me that your cares and love are my most treasured possessions, a desideratum priceless, a spark that signified the difference between joyful living and mere existence. At times, I might have been a fool. War is a serious business and has taught me the serious side of life; so when I return to you it'll be in the guise of a sadder, but wiser man."

To summarize it all, I wish to apologize for my tantrums; I promise to love and cherish you; to make you a happy woman; to add to your life what the war has subtracted; to be a kind and sympathetic husband and father.

October 2, 1944

I enjoyed those snapshots of you and the kids. Here you are the Mother of our 2 girls and your looks & figure resemble a young, pretty gal. I have a confession to make. As I kept gazing at your picture, I longed to take you in my arms and hold you. It seems so long ago and so far away that I sometimes wonder why must such joys be denied us.

I miss your love and care; I miss your companionship. With you near me I was at peace. I'm proud of you too because you are taking it on the chin. You are suffering silently and elegantly while many others think the world owes them their husbands at a time like this. I have often remarked that I have given the best years of my wife to the Army.

A new day is dawning though. It may perhaps not appear too near, yet, it surely is not far off. When that day will break it'll find us hand in hand, facing people proudly. When we'll look into the free and happy faces of children we'll think: Our sacrifices were worth all this.

I'm proud to be in combat and I know you're proud for me.

October 4, 1944

Last night was the coldest one since our arrival here. Most of us now wear the long woolen undies. They might look comical, but are a sure comfort and almost a necessity in these cow pastures.

After finishing work at 7 this morning I breakfasted & then had to wait for my barber's appointment… There's only one barber and he's a busy man. He only cuts hair and the charge is 20 francs = 40 cents. After that I took a shower in our portable shower unit. At least that's one advantage in being with a hospital unit.

The Army also has mobile shower units, but in actual combat it's not possible to operate. We've had patients who for over 60 days have slept in foxholes, pup tents, no showers, and have eaten the K or C rations.

The cold though is the worst of all and the hardest to endure. It's tough on the doctors, but tougher on the wounded. Some early mornings the operating tent is very cold.

October 5, 1944

While I read about plans how the civilians back home will celebrate V-Day and the Army's Demobilization Plan our wounded continue to stream in. So it is with a cynical eye that I ponder over such premature reports…

Actually, the local stalemate seems to have been broken. Our wounded have just told me that more Nazi strongpoints have been taken. We know here very well that the fighting will get tougher in Germany proper. In addition to the military resistance, we'll have a hostile population to contend with, whereas in France, Belgium, Holland & Luxembourg the vast majority of the civilians cheered and welcomed us.

October 6, 1944

You'll probably read and hear much about our present campaign. The sector our troops are attacking bristles with huge fortifications whose walls of steel and concrete might measure over 19 inches thick and over 40 feet deep.

Last night I was talking with a wounded Lt. who had been on top of one of these large forts. Our men had not been able to get into it although they had stormed the top. The Nazis merely stick below where they have plenty of food & ammunition. We are trying to force them out by pouring oil down the air-vents & then setting them on fire.

The Huns have plenty of heavy artillery.... Our air force has had little favorable weather thus far. Our infantry is meeting tougher opposition since the Nazis have good troops in this sector. They have not used foreigners....who try not to fight when the going gets tough and often have surrendered to us.

October 8, 1944

We are finally beginning to get some sunny days after so much rain and cloudiness. The clear skies are also a great help to our doughboys for then our planes can blast away at the powerful enemy fortifications.

A few days ago I had as a patient a wounded Austrian. He told me that the Austrians are disgusted, that the Nazis had deceived them and had appropriated most of the property and possessions to themselves. He further stated that the German civilians have little food and want the war to end, but are afraid to say anything. Germans who grumbled after the heavy RAF raids were either shot or placed in the dreaded concentration camp.

October 9, 1944

The sunshine only lasted for 2 days. Now it's again cloudy and chilly. I guess this will keep our planes grounded.

The Special Service Division of the Army and Navy with the Red Cross are showing us movies... The film tent is so crowded that it's almost impossible to get a seat. Even those who might have seen the picture 2 or even 3 times remain for want of anything else to do at night. Last night I had to stand to see "Step Lively" with Frank Sinatra. Every time the voice sang the soldiers would mimic, "oh Frankie" so a good time was had by all.

Last night a Frenchmen came in. I discovered that he spoke German so I engaged him in conversation and learned some interesting stories.

He is a native of the province of Lorraine which had been directly incorporated into Germany proper after the defeat of France in 1940. The black market was a thriving business, maintained and encouraged by the Nazi officials; especially the Gestapo, SS and the office-holders.

Each member of the family was permitted one chicken per year. Its eggs also belonged to the owner. For every other chicken, 60 eggs per year had to be sold to the Nazis --- at the conqueror's price, of course. They were allowed 2 glasses of milk per child under 14. Adults were permitted one glass. Only 2 cigarettes per day were permissible.

Russian prisoners worked in the nearby mines and were horribly treated. A day before the Americans freed the town, the Nazis removed the Russians…

October 10, 1944

I've been thinking about the war bonds. I've forgotten the exact figures, but our total thus far must be over $1200. That and the future bonds will be for the children's education.

It's drizzly and cloudy now so again the activity of our planes will be limited. These dam Nazis have luck. On clear days we can blast away at them and thus prevent their supplies and reinforcements from reaching the front.

Last night I admitted a 35 year old German PW in civilian clothing. He was brought to us from the PW stockade. He told me the following story:

He's been ill and in the German Army it's difficult to see a doctor. The aidman handles everything. He noticed how the Nazi officers were drunk often and plundered, sending the spoils to their families in Germany.

Well, they were ordered to the front, put in position and told to hold at all costs. Their officers then left them; so here were the Huns with only the NCO's (Sgt., etc.) enduring cold, rain, hunger, our air and artillery fire.

He claimed that many of the Huns picked up our surrender leaflets (which our planes drop on their lines urging them to give up the useless struggle and guaranteeing safe passage) and would have liked to surrender. They fear however, the consequences to their families in Germany.

Just picture an army educated to the obsession of a super race, supermen, super arms & every other super-duper. For 4 years they've been able to dish it out and their one track brains have been drilled with the myth that the Nazis will always dish it out to others and won't have to take it.

Then the first break in their thick skulls occurs. The terrific bombings of the American & RAF planes cow and terrify the German civilians. The Gestapo acts swiftly and mercilessly. Any German grumbling or complaining is either shot or imprisoned.

The soldiers themselves however, still are far away and eating well. Suddenly, all hell breaks loose! Our planes, artillery, armor and even our Navy overwhelm them. The Huns are told by their officers that the Luftwaffe will arrive, that supplies and reinforcements will come, that above all, the flying bombs and other secret weapons are on the way.

The Nazi soldiers wait, wait in vain. The PWs have told me that the disgusted Hun soldiers would see our planes in the air and sarcastically remark "unsere (our) Luftwaffe." The Hun soldiers also notice the haughtiness of their officers.

Yes, the ordinary Jerry soldier would like to quit for his thick shell has finally realized that the brutal Nazi game will soon be up. Well, what keeps him in line? In my opinion it's the aforementioned fear; fear for his family, the brutal Gestapo consequences.

So most of these men fight on & on. The Nazi political troops, the SS troops or those fanatically loyal to Hitler are in every German unit, threatening to shoot any German soldier who'll give up and also threating to report any quitter to the Gestapo who'll then care for his family in the Nazi manner.

The German soldier I mentioned was a Sgt. and with 4 men was posted in an observation outpost. He sent his men on missions and deserted to a house where an elderly woman befriended him, gave him civilian clothing and hid him for 3 weeks until the Americans entered the town and he surrendered to us voluntarily.

Of course, all such stories must be checked. Plenty of Germans and fascist civilians from these occupied countries changed into civilian clothing & remained behind to spy on the Allies. I myself know of such an instance.

When the full story of the Nazi barbarism and atrocities will be told the world will shudder.

October 13, 1944

I've just returned from the operating room where I assisted....in a brain case. This soldier had shrapnel penetrate his brain. On the way to the O.R. he stopped breathing so both Jimmy & I worked on him until he began to breathe again and we then hurried to try to remove the blood clots & destroyed brain matter & shattered bone which were pressing on his brain. After the operation we still had to observe him carefully. As yet we can't say whether he'll make it despite all our efforts.

October 14, 1944

Our C.O. told me to speak to our PWs concerning the regulations they are to adhere to so all of them were gathered and I spoke in German to them. I'm trying to learn some French, but it's rather difficult in this environment.

October 19, 1944

I never realized that I'd be serving also in the Navy; but here I am, believe it or not, living in 6 inches of water, surrounded by water, and every time I tried to walk from one area of the field to another I'd have to cross 10 – 12 inches of water.

The Army paper, the Stars & Stripes states that France is now experiencing the worst autumn weather in 80 years. This morning the inside of our tent was full of water. We slushed around in the tent, each telling the other what to do, laughing like hyenas at our own expense. These cynical outbursts of laughter kept us in stiches. It really was a case of laugh clown laugh.

All day we kept digging, pumping, bailing water and enlarging the outside ditches. The rain continued & pretty soon whatever water we poured out of the tent seeped back.

Our trucks with some PWs brought sand. We repaired the overtaxed irrigation ditches. We had a deep hole dug in the tent & drained the inside water. Finally the PWs covered the ground with sand, leaving the big hole inside for drainage.

The wind was so terrific during the past 2 nights that I thought our tent would collapse. Some were on the verge of caving in. Last night my Receiving tent was flapped around for hours and almost was floored. One of the nearby Evacuation hospitals was washed out.

We've had to pitch large Ward tents to accommodate our officer personnel who've been washed out of their Pyramidal tents in which 4 live. The Ward tents quarter about 18 – 20 persons dormitory style. I'll know by the morning whether all the repairs have made our tent habitable. Otherwise, we too will join in the dormitory before we float over.

Our sense of humor is unimpaired. Rain or shine we'll continue to grin. Our shoes, pants, raincoats, etc. look like walking mud. Fortunately it hasn't been unbearably cold. This morning the officers' latrine was half blown down. I had to climb through the top canvas to get in while the wind almost blew me out. We have lots of fun though. One gets used to mud, water, etc.

October 21, 1944

We've managed to dry out our tent ground fairly well with our irrigation ditches and deep holes. From time to time we remove the accumulated water in these holes with buckets. The outside ground is however, hopelessly water-logged, slushy, muddy and just pools of deep gooey mud.

Yesterday I made a trip to a real city, outside of France. Signs all over proclaimed, "Welcome to our liberator". Street cars were running and private autos with coke generators furnishing the power instead of the scarce gasoline were evident everywhere. This big town was hardly touched by the war.

It felt grand to get away from the mud, see clean streets, walk on clean sidewalks and see cleanly dressed people. It just makes the environment we had left back home dearer.

The news about the fall of the German stronghold of Aachen was most welcome here. After this stalemate the capture of Aachen, Belgrade in Yugoslavia, & the Russian advances in E. Prussia, renewed our hopes for a quicker victory. It's hell to fight in mud & rain. Just imagine a winter campaign!

Anyways, I thought of her *(daughter, Sylvia)* today, just one year old. I wonder how she'll react to me when I'll return. Will she scream like her sister did, "don't touch Mommy"?

October 25, 1944

Here we are again in a new location, still in France. There was only one reason for this movement and that was mud. We were so bogged down that it almost became impossible to operate. We had to get out before our vehicles would also get stuck. All in all it was an awful mess.

We dreaded the movement for that meant getting our val-packs, bed rolls & tents full of mud. This fear was obviated however, by having the trucks drive up to the tent and having the PW's carry the luggage and loading it instead of first piling it on the ground, as per custom.

The new location is picturesque, way up on a hill with a grand view of the surrounding country and villages. Theoretically, any excess rainfall should easily drain off in the valley below.

October 30, 1944

I'm on the night shift this week and therefore, have to sleep on a litter in the Receiving tent during the lull --- as soon as patients arrive I'm up. It got so cold at about 2 a.m. that I awoke shivering and suffered for 2 hours from the cold. The 2 ovens had gotten stone cold. This is just another one of the shivering experiences I've felt in the Army.

Charlie … and I walked down to the nearby village in the afternoon. The people wore their Sunday best and for the most part were friendly. Since we are nearer to Germany now we can't expect the same type of enthusiasm the Frenchmen exhibited in France proper.

Two mornings ago I was dressing when I heard a peculiar harsh drone. Soon men outside began to shout "buzz bomb = flying bomb" overhead. We looked out and sure enough there was this buzzer with its typical flame-spouting tail speeding over us. Fortunately it sped out of sight. We don't know where it landed. This was the first flying bomb I had actually seen in operation.

October 31, 1944

Some time ago we were not far from the French town of Verdun, the scene of the bloodiest fighting of the last war. Only a small part of it was in ruins as the Nazis were forced to withdraw hurriedly.

The city has a huge monument and contains many fortresses. A few of us toured one of them which must have been at least 100 feet deep with many winding tunnels and very thick walls. After viewing these old forts I can readily appreciate the tremendous difficulties involved in attacking modern constructed fortifications like those around Metz or the Siegfried Line.

When we visit French towns…we may go to restaurants or cafes, but the Army forbids us from buying in food stores and rightly so. The civilians need such food, we don't. Our own mess feeds us more than enough.

Our PW's were taken away from us by order of Army authorities and returned to our stockades. I'm convinced…that only combat troops, i.e. those who've fought it out with the Nazis, should guard them. Non-combat personnel are too darn soft on these supermen who take quick advantage of the leniency shown them by the democratic countries. We are not firm enough with these Nazis soldiers who soon try to ingratiate themselves into our favor with their assumed innocence and good fellowship. I've even seen & heard a PW offer a cigarette to an American soldier with these words "have one, Comrade."

November 2, 1944

When dawn broke yesterday morning we found the dew had frozen. Most of us wear the long woolen underwear, undershirt & drawers, and 2 pairs of socks --- cotton next to the feet & over it the heavy woolen ones. I even wear cotton underwear beneath the woolies as this minimizes any itching… and also adds to warmth.

If it weren't for the QM mobile laundry, we'd really be in difficulty trying to wash woolens in helmets & pails… Thank heavens we may send 20 pieces of laundry weekly which is washed, but not ironed. Our woolen trousers & top shirts are pressed by one of our men for 40 cents.

At present we only get coke to fire the stoves. Coke will only burn in a hot fire & is therefore, good to bank the stove. Otherwise it's hard to start a good fire with it. We hope to get coal soon.

November 3, 1944

We've had little rain in this area. Even if we did we are fairly well prepared with gravel all over the place. I guess I'll never forget the mud in our previous area and especially the days our tent floor (ground) was covered with six inches of water. No combat soldier ever forgets the mud.

Another month has gone by, another month nearer to those I miss most. We just exist here for the days to pass into weeks, the weeks to months, and the latter to bring us to the rich life some maniacs have deprived us of – not for long we hope.

November 6, 1944

Yesterday I received a V-letter from… I must have written him to the effect that the people back home should realize that this war is tougher than they believe and ought to exert more effort. I quote his reply: "You seem to have a low opinion of your countrymen back home, but they are not as bad as you think. A lot of us are trying to do everything possible and many of us would prefer being there, helping to get rid of that beastly scourge."

When I read this remark to my tent mates we all chorused "Baloney". Most of those guys crying that they would "prefer to be there" are just putting on an act. Soldiers become hard, very realistic and brutally frank. We would prefer a man to tell the truth than boast in an empty manner.

November 9, 1944

The rains still are bearing down on us at frequent intervals and one walks in mud --- although it's still a paradise as compared to our previous area. We've had to revise our irrigation plans and construct some new ditches to carry off the excess rainfall.

In front of the Receiving tent a miniature lake has been formed. My practical Sgt. hung up a sign "No fishing". My men are out there now, picks & shovels in hand, digging a new drainage ditch.

To prevent the dripping from the tent canvas over my bed, I strung up a sort of canopy with my pup tent canvas. Now the water drops on it and I have it tilted so that the flow is over my bed.

As I write many of our heavy bombers are in the skies. We can hear the explosions of their dropped bombs. It's a beautiful sight to watch; especially when these bomber formations are friendly ones.

November 10, 1944

We were quite busy all day yesterday with many casualties. Our attack yesterday gained much ground. The Nazis had planted many land mines & booby traps. One of our men told me that a few weeks ago his outfit came across a dead Nazi with his watch exposed. A keen-eyed American soldier noticed wire running up his arm. This dead Hun had been booby trapped by his own men… I've heard where severely wounded Nazis, whom the supermen expect to die anyway, were booby trapped. One of them waved away and American aid man coming to help.

November 11, 1944

Today is Armistice Day, but I guess it's just a grim reminder that the 1918 armistice was actually a 21 year one and nothing else.

Here we're very busy again. All last night our big guns kept roaring, casualties are pouring in. Many Nazi PWs are amongst them and I've been told that many more are waiting in our PW enclaves for transportation back to our hospitals.

We got a wounded Hun 2nd Lt. who cussed Hitler. Of course, all such anti-Nazi manifestations by German soldiers are to be taken with a grain of salt. They have ulterior motives expecting us to give them better care if they now denounce Shickelgruber.

Today is the first clear day in over a week. The rains & mud have been heavy up to now. The nights & mornings quite cold so that we're not only fighting the enemy, but the weather and the mud, mud, mud.

The pleasures of watching them *(his two girls)* grow up have been denied me. I have however, the pleasure of knowing that I'm part of a great Army struggling to make all such pleasures possible without fear of concentration camps or fascism.

November 13, 1944

I understand that many or most of the airmail letters have been sent here via ships. The planes were full of high priority items and just couldn't spare the precious space for letters. This situation will probably continue as we'll always need more food, medicines & ammunition.

I've just been conversing with some of the infantry soldiers we've been admitting. One told me that his company had to wade through water to attack. Actually it wasn't too much of a hindrance as the floods forced the Huns to come out of the cellars, dugouts, etc. His outfit suffered many casualties from land-mines.

Many of the men coming in suffer from the so-called Trench foot. This condition is caused by long exposure in a damp cold, especially in trenches and is a milder form of frostbite.

The electric generators have again been repaired and so again we have electric light in our tents. What a blessing that is --- candles are such a poor substitute.

November 14, 1944

Tonight it began to snow and in the drier areas the snow remained solid making it the first snowfall of the season. The front lines are flooded, full of mud, snow & ice. The nights are very dark. Ambulances have a real tough time driving through the dark slush and mud with their dim (blacked-out) lights. The wounded arrive cold & full of mud & filth.

I wish you'd be able to get a telephone installed *(my Mother has now been waiting at least 2 months)*. Perhaps if you continue reminding the company…stressing the fact that you are alone with 2 kids.

November 16, 1944

We've been most busy these past 24 hours. At times we didn't have enough beds to accommodate many of the patients. It wasn't so much the wounds as the exposure to the snow, sleet & mud. As soon as we could evacuate a case his bed was grabbed for another patient.

A wounded soldier told me that a Nazi patrol of about 7 men came across 8 American wounded soldiers. The leader spoke English and asked the first wounded American for a box of chocolate. The American said he had none; the Nazi shot him dead & sprayed the 5 others with bullets. The one telling me the story had his face covered & played dead so the Huns thinking he really was gone merely kicked him in the neck. Later he was picked up by our litter bearers. Our men are fighting mad.

November 17, 1944

Many of our patients arrive in mud-soaked, wet clothing. The ground is just covered with mud, snow & slush and the combat soldiers & wounded must lie on it. Mud and war are synonymous. Once our heavy vehicles begin to traverse the water logged ground we can expect general mud.

Even though you write that this dentist is still at Fort Dix I'm not envious. One look at our wounded, our tired, muddy, filthy, rain soaked soldiers and I became proud to be near them, happy that I can be where I'm really needed supporting their heroic struggles. Most people back home will never surmise what our men go through.

No, watching movies, reading or looking at war pictures can never really make you truly appraise a combat soldier's sacrifices. It's quite a difference to experience rain, shivering cold, knee-deep mud, filth, living in the field, consuming Army rations, being exposed to the exigencies of combat, let alone the deprivations of your accustomed way of life and absence from the family.

November 19, 1944

We've been having hectic days here with the wounded pouring in and our evacuation channels overloaded with patients. In order to accommodate all the Trench feet cases we had to rush cots & blankets into the movie tent which is now a ward.

Our soldiers were beating the Nazis back, but the struggle was tough. The Huns had their big guns zeroed in on all the roads we had to traverse and their snipers were all over. The fighting was therefore, bitter and costly and dirty.

The latter is reflected in the feelings of our soldiers who tell me that the Nazis are "dirty fighters" and cuss them. When our wounded see Nazis admitted to the hospital they exclaim, "before they were out to kill us now we treat them".

I admitted 2 badly wounded delirious Nazis. We had a hell of a time getting their stinking clothes off & when this was done lice were crawling all over them. Lots of the Army delousing powder was sprinkled on them.

Some of the Nazi officers think they're a highly privileged class. Even the Nazi non-commissioned officers; especially the various grades of Sgts, have soldier orderlies. I heard a story that a bunch of Nazi prisoners were being loaded into a truck. A Hun 1st Sgt. refused to get in with the ordinary Nazi soldiers. Our MPs made up his mind.

Some of our soldiers haven't taken off their clothing in 2 – 4 weeks. Many haven't had a hot meal for days and subsist on the K or C rations. The company kitchen really tries hard to get hot meals to the front-line men, but often it becomes an impossibility.

The morale of our men is excellent. This particular division is really fighting mad and they're resolved to carry out their onerous task successfully.

I wonder what it'll feel like to undress in a civilized house, take a shower, jump into a soft bed and then take you in my arms. I'll bet it'll be a heaven to men all over, men whose wives are as lovely as mine. I'll make it up to you for all your love, devotion and lonely waiting.

November 21, 1944

The hectic days continue and yesterday we were flooded with Nazis. Our troops had captured a Nazi hospital and all their wounded poured in and I was swamped with interpretations. Two German civilian policemen were brought in. When we placed the wounded record forms on him, he looked and in a quivering & nervous voice began to plead with me that he's 47 years old, has a family, is not a Nazi & is not to blame, so please have mercy on him. When I asked the reason for this outburst he said that the words "Transportation" --- routine printed words on all records --- made him think that he was marked for punishment. I told him about the Nazi atrocities. I heard that the Nazis surrendered a fort recently; 300 Huns marched out & soon after the American soldiers entered the fort was blown by the Nazis.

November 23, 1944

By now all the men have been issued overshoes and that helps keep the feet dry. Recently I had to go on a reconnaissance tour with our Colonel. We passed through many flooded areas. In one region the water reached the top of the jeep wheels.

We passed through much destruction and we could easily see why the Nazis were able to make a strong stand. I saw row upon row of Nazi dugouts, pill-houses, block- houses & gun positions. The larger ones were covered with grass and had a foot of stovepipe sticking out. They faced the strategic roads and many fields were mined and bobby-trapped.

Our jeep stopped and I began to question an 18 year old civilian about the roads.

He replied in French so I asked him if he spoke German and in that language he informed us that a certain bridge we had to cross was blown up. We there-fore, detoured finally reaching our destination. Someday I'll tell you more of the interesting story when it'll no longer be censorable.

Yesterday afternoon we were again flooded with sick and wounded Nazis. I quizzed one of them who volunteered to talk about the atrocities. Here are some of them:

French patriots whom the Germans termed "terrorists" were caught. Over 1200 of them were crowded together and placed in a cattle train, 100 crammed into a cattle car, locked tight, and for the 1000 mile trip to Austria --- I don't know how many days it took --- were not let out once or fed. When they reached their destination over a third of these Frenchmen were dead.

Soon after the Nazis stormed into Russia and had captured Kiev, they crowd-ed all the Jews there into a ghetto, had the stronger Hebrews dig large ditches in the suburbs then loaded many of the Jews onto wagons --- babies, children, grandmothers, etc. --- and drove them out there. They were then forced to kneel in these ditches while the Huns shot them. Details then poured a disinfectant over the fallen ones & buried them. It didn't make any difference whether these poor Jews were really dead or still alive. The earth was thrown over them and that was all. Such bestialities were repeated daily.

Incidentally, one of the reserve policemen who had participated in such atrocities & who had related this story to my informer, also a policeman, had suffered a nervous breakdown. He claimed that he was forced to do such heinous crimes because he was afraid to protest to his officers.

Of course, the Gestapo & other Nazi bigwigs had ordered the policeman we had captured to fight to the last bullets, but they themselves took off towards Germany. Our troops however, captured many of them. As far as I'm concerned any Gestapo or SS Nazi should be tried & killed.

November 24, 1944

Yesterday we celebrated Thanksgiving Day by carrying on just the same, but the dinner at 1 p.m. was a gala event. We had real turkey, stuffing, cranberry sauce, cole slaw, apple pie, coke, green peas, potatoes, cheese, candy, apples, cigars, cigarettes & coffee --- a $2.50 dinner if there ever were one and it tasted swell. Everyone ate to the saturation point and any soldier not exactly in an isolated combat position ate turkey.

November 28, 1944

This evening I had a patient, a 39 year old Russian civilian... He was enslaved by the Nazis and forced to work in the coal mines in Lorraine province where he was paid 6 marks = $2.40 on the old rate of exchange, per month. All the Russian prisoners were fed bread and soup daily and in addition they could buy 2 quarts beer and 1/8 lb. tobacco monthly. They slept on straw beds, triple decker, with one blanket and the barracks was never heated. The Huns worked them 8 hours daily – I guess it was not humanly possible to work longer in the mines or the Huns would have made them do so. About 15 Russians died daily. The one Russian doctor was given very few drugs for treating these workmen. This Russian was suffering from malnutrition. Oh yes! He was allowed 2 baths a month.

November 30, 1944

We continue to be busy out here. Last night was a humdinger. At least 75 Nazi PWs were admitted to our hospital in about 2 hours. One of the Hun forts finally surrendered so all their wounded were sent to us while the others were taken to the PW enclosures.

When they were brought in…the odor and stench were nauseating. They really stunk-up the Receiving Ward, the Surgical Ward and the Operating Room --- and I'm not exaggerating.

Our C.O. sat alongside of me as I was interviewing these Heinies and extracted some interesting information from them. As a matter of fact, quite a few officers like to sit near me when I interview the PWs…

The men told me that they had enough food for one day more and that their ammunition was very low. Their daily rations consisted of: 1 ½ lbs. bread, 1/4 lb. wurst, 1/16 lb. schmaltz, 1 quart soup, 6 – 10 cigarettes daily.

The toilet was on the outside of the fort and the Americans had it surrounded so the Huns had to do their natural chores right near their bunks. They told me that the stink was overpowering, their morale rock bottom.

We've had a few 4F plus PWs. The one we had last night was a 58 year old … who was ordered to active duty after 2 days of training in the use of the machine gun and small arms. He suffered from shortness of breath & was sickly looking. This old man had never been a soldier and stated that prison or death awaited him if he refused the call to arms. Men from 16 – 60 years are drafted…

Daily we're learning more and more of the Nazi cruelties. Our infantry men know how treacherous they can be in combat and how "sweet & innocent" they act when in captivity. It's the usual story. The SS and the Gestapo and the party are guilty, but we poor, little people of Germany are innocent. We in the combat groups cannot and will not be fooled by such devilish arguments. The politicians should remember this. Nazism must be ruthlessly annihilated for only then can the dignity of mankind reassert itself.

December 5, 1944

My letters often described the difficulties of running a tent-hospital in winter. The difficulties caused by the cold, rain and mud were often too severe not only on the personnel, but especially on the patients.

All Evacuation hospitals in the 3rd Army --- perhaps this is also true of the other Armies --- were ordered to be sheltered in buildings. When I went on that reconnaissance trip with the Colonel it was for the purpose of finding a hospital which the Germans had used.

Well, we finally got a place of our own, rather near to Germany. Today we moved and as our luck would go it was a rainy, windy day and it also hailed. We sat in an open truck and really felt these annoyances. Of course, I can't tell you how far we are or how long we travelled. The important item is that at long last we're now inside solid walls after 7 months of living in tents.

December 6, 1944

The buildings we're using are old & rather worn. As the war moved nearer to Germany, the Nazis moved their PWs to Germany & used it as a hospital. Now we took over and had to salvage whatever remains.

As would happen, the building Salami Haven is quartered in is ice cold. It has central heating, but the boiler is defective & we don't know how long it'll take to fix it.

There are about 10 rooms in the one story building, three of which are occupied by Colonels. The latter of course, had stoves installed in their rooms prior to their occupancy. The rest of us have to wait. All in all there's lots of repairing, altering & reorganization before things will straighten out completely, for the Huns left this area in bad shape.

In accordance with Army permission we are hiring civilian help; especially, those employed by the Germans after they are investigated by the French for collaboration, etc. They are necessary to run our enlarged hospital.

As we approach nearer to Germany we are getting nearer to the end. It'll still be a tough battle while it lasts, but it's getting shorter and for that matter less waiting for us.

December 12, 1944

Gradually our hospital is taking shape. The boiler in our living quarters has been repaired so we're getting some heat in the room. Only one of our radiators is working, the other one needs repairing, but at least even a small amount of heat removes the chill from the room.

We're still having lots of rain. If we could only have sunny and balmy days for the next 2 – 3 weeks, the war would certainly end sooner. The rain & clouds not only impede our troops & vehicles, but our air force. The Nazis therefore, have the chance to dig in and fortify themselves.

December 16, 1944

Yesterday I walked over to gaze upon a gruesome site. Not far from us was a new Jewish cemetery which had a few graves. The Nazis desecrated it, knocked down the monuments…opened the graves which were enlarged to a depth of 9 ft., 10 ft. long and 7 ft. wide and filled with Russian dead.

These were the Russian workers & soldiers whom they starved & worked to death. Only a numbered wooden sign marks the top of each mound which contains at least 150 bodies per. Our civilian guide told us that the Russians were buried naked, lime poured over them & then soil.

There was a putrefying stench over the huge graves & mounds as the rains had washed off the top soil & left 8 inches to cover the top bodies. Not too far away is another burial ground where 20,000 Russians are buried…

December 18, 1944

Casualties keep arriving, all testifying to the toughness and bitterness of the struggle. The Nazis not only have powerful pillboxes, but have fortified many buildings which our troops have to blast open.

I'm feeling fine, in good spirits and glad that I'm able to do my bit for our troops whom we can never repay. Keep the home fires burning…

December 20, 1944

My room is still cold, but there's not much I can do about it. By spreading another blanket under my bed roll I manage to get some added protection from the bed-spring. We have no mattresses, but by this time I'm used to such discomforts and sleep on anything.

XMAS 1944

Everyone of us, excluding the men at the very front, had a special dinner. When we approached the chow line our mess gears were loaded with turkey, stuffing, mashed potatoes, asparagus, cranberry sauce, cabbage salad and coffee. For dessert we ate canned peaches, fresh apples and were each given 1 Hershey bar, 1 pack cigarettes and 1 cigar.

It was a well-cooked and really delicious meal even though most of it had to be eaten in one dish. However, we're so used to lumping all our food together that it now makes very little difference. The booming of the artillery reminded us though that the fighting was not too far off and that other soldiers weren't as fortunate as we were in having a fine meal.

You'll probably hear plenty about the latest Nazi offensive. Just bear this in mind, when we attack we must fight over terrain which has powerful & fixed defenses and over many mine-fields. The Nazis do not have to worry about mines & fixed defenses when they rush to the offensive since the only time an army mines the roads & prepares fixed positions, like forts, is when it's on the defensive or for the purpose of defense.

The Huns therefore, can advance 30 – 40 miles during their offensive while we recover from the initial assault. We are confident here that the attack will be stopped and as General Eisenhower says, "by coming out in the open the foe gives us the chance of destroying him."

There are no illusions here, perhaps as might exist amongst some people in the U.S.A. The U.S. troops here know that it'll be a hard struggle for a few months more. Have no fears, all continues satisfactory despite this momentary set-back. I have the same faith in our inevitable victory as I have of returning to you & our children --- for you are my fondest dream, hopes and happiness.

December 26, 1944

It's the day after Xmas, a clear, sunny and brisk day. The ground we tread on is hard and frozen solid. Gone is the mud of yesterday, where the soil was too watery a mass of ice covers it.

We can't draw water from the faucets of the Lister bags on the water trailers as they are frozen. Instead we must climb on top of the tank, open the lid and draw the water & ice into our canteens and helmets or basins. The local water, and that means in the buildings we occupy, is contaminated so the Army supplies us with its own chlorinated water.

Our planes are out in full force. We gaze at the skies proudly and know this fine weather will really help turn the present battle in our favor. The rest you'll probably read in the papers or listen to the radio.

I bought a sweater from the Quartermaster Officers' store. It is 100% wool and costs about $3. Now I'm all set for the winter weather… These sweaters are long sleeved, high (buttoned) neck and are issued to the soldiers, except officers who buy all their clothing.

The civilian electrician who repaired the electricity in our buildings … spoke French & German --- most people in these parts speak both languages. I learned that he had an extra small radio he was willing to sell. He preferred canned goods so I made a deal with him as we had more canned stuff than we could eat. Now I have a swell, small, short-wave radio to bring us news & music. I get the BBC & ABSiE (American Broadcasting Station in Europe) & many other stations…

December 30, 1944

Since it's been officially announced over the radio that General Patton's 3rd Army was attacking the German offensive, I may now add certain information which was heretofore censorable.

When the Nazi attack was making good progress we were rather near the German lines… The Army didn't know exactly where we would be needed so they decided to put us in Metz for a few days.

So although we were about 25 miles beyond Metz we moved the entire hospital on Dec. 23rd to the capital city of the province of Lorraine. We stayed in Metz for a few days. Our rooms had some steam, but the plumbing was out of order so we dug an outside latrine in a tent and carried water into our rooms.

We had an excellent Xmas turkey dinner and then were allowed passes to roam the city of Metz. Metz has a population of about 100,000 and like any European city has its old sections and its new sections.

Some edifices date back to the 16th century and many buildings have Gothic and Byzantine (Turkish) architecture. Most of the city suffered little damage… Metz was surrounded and protected by some of the most formidable forts in the world. These fortifications held up our advance from Sept. – Nov.

Up to 1870 Alsace-Lorraine belonged to France. After the Franco-Prussian War (1870 – 1871) Germany took it away from France and kept it until 1919 when the Treaty of Versailles returned it to France. When the Nazis invaded French territory in 1940 they annexed Alsace-Lorraine outright. So you see why these 2 provinces bordering between France & Germany and speaking both languages are a problem. Some civilians are naturally unfriendly as they are Germans; others are probably afraid, but we haven't been as well received here as in France proper.

I'll close with the wish that 1945 may find us together in our blue heaven.

Fourteen

1945, MOVING TOWARD VICTORY

*F*rance, Belgium, Germany, Czechoslovakia, the 109th Evacuation Hospital constant-ly seemed to be racing to keep up with the Third Army. January marked four years that Dad had been on active military duty. He believed that victory in Europe was close, even as the fighting continued and the casualties poured in. He was weary of war and longed to return to his family. However, despite this and a personal disappointment, he still was happy to serve his country and treat its soldiers.

He was very angry over the Nazi's treatment of American POWs and the atrocities he heard about. At this point he knew about the German concentration camps, but I don't know if he realized the full extent of the Holocaust. I wish I had questioned him about that when he was alive. He saw the terrific destruction that the Allied Air Force had done to German cities. Displaced refugees from areas liberated by the Allies were wandering through Europe searching for anything that might sustain them as they tried to make their way back home.

The 109th was the first Third Army Evacuation Hospital to cross the Rhine River into Germany. Victory in Europe was declared on May 8, 1945 and Dad finally returned to the United States about two months later.

Germany, 1945

Frankfurt, March 1945, bomb
damage

Captured German warehouse, April, 1945
near Nuremberg

In Front of an Evacuation Hospital (location & date
unknown) Captain Cantor, 2nd row, 3rd from left

Fifteen

January 1, 1945

In a few days a new location was chosen for us, so again we packed and were off to help support our counter-attack to the latest Nazi offensive. I can't tell you where we are now.

We're using French buildings to quarter the patients & staff. When we first arrived very few of the buildings had steam and these stone structures can be plenty cold. Now most of the radiators have been fixed so it's comfortable.

Our quarters though have non-functioning radiators… The plumbing is in poor shape. The accommodations generally are bad. The litter bearers have to haul patients to certain wards which are 2 flights up through rather narrow doorways.

Again we've hired French civilians to work around the hospitals… The buildings we usually find are rather filthy & neglected.

The surrounding countryside is blanketed with a thin snow and frost. It's better than the mud and I hope it'll stay so. Our troops can maneuver better.

Our soldiers feel optimistic about throwing von Rundsted's latest offensive back. We've made quite some headway since the Nazi offensive began. The cold adds to the hardships of all the soldiers.

All's well otherwise. I hope that the next year will find us reunited to enjoy our children and plan ahead for their welfare. I realize that it's harder on you than on me. This "enforced-loneliness" will not last much longer and after that I'll do my utmost to make you happy.

January 2, 1945

I have never complained about the promotion business to those back home so this is only for your consumption. As far as I'm concerned, I've been given a raw deal. By all standards and in fairness I should have received a promotion. You know my length of service and overseas duty. Instead of fairness, our C.O. double-crossed a few of the deserving and promoted an officer who's been a boot-licker and the least capable. Quite a few of the officers are disgusted and down in the dumps over the unfairness and incompetence in our outfit.

In the Army however, we have to swallow a lot. After all, as doctors we strive for the welfare of the patients and disregard our personal gripes. It wasn't the fact that I personally didn't receive the promotion. If it had gone to other deserving officers none of us would care. But when a boot-licker & incompetent man gets the reward and in addition, is one of our youngest, least trained doctors with about 2 years of Army service it's disgusting.

I celebrated New Year's eve in my room by listening to the radio... Hitler spoke at 12:05 a.m. so I tried to listen to his speech in which he promised a German victory in 6 months. I'm sure the Nazis will recall his former vain promises.

Don't forget though that this discouragement of mine applies only to what I've mentioned. I'm glad to be here to do my bit for our soldiers. I've always said that benefits come to me the hard way. Perhaps my reward will come later.

I know what the soldiers endure, especially, in this type of fighting and in this freezing weather. I've seen their feet swollen and black and blue from the frost. I've seen some ghastly wounds. Do you therefore, wonder that I consider it a privilege to serve our men? We all have our gripes, but not all of us have the satisfaction of doing your part.

Here are some interesting highlights about the German offensive into Belgium:

The Nazis attacked with lots of American equipment and many Germans wore American uniforms over their German dress. These disguised vehicles — according to the Geneva Convention enemy soldiers not fighting in their proper uniforms may be considered as spies and shot --- rode through our lines & disrupted our communications by cutting telephone wires, etc.

Two of our officers saw an American tank followed by 2 American armored vehicles about ¼ mile away. A jeep drove by and warned them that it was really a German manned tank. Soon 2 of our anti-tank guns got direct hits on the apparently American armor. Later when examination was possible it was discovered that all the occupants of this tank were Nazis. How some of our men knew about this Nazi trick is a mystery, but the results counted.

January 3, 1945

You express fear in your last letter --- fear of the war. Actually you should feel proud because I'm proud to serve here and you must take pride in the noble sacrifice your domestic life has to endure. We must be certain that all children shall have the inalienable right to enjoy the freedoms.

I've always said that the nearest thing to death is to exist under Nazi tyranny. The latter can never be destroyed by mere talk. These sacrifices we now make will annihilate Hitlerism and anyone participating in this gigantic struggle ought to feel proud.

Keep your head and spirits high for we'll be able to say "We were there and did our share."

January 4, 1945

Our soldiers are becoming raving mad at the Nazis. As one infantry Lt. said, "The Nazis use all kinds of dirty tricks while we try to fight the American way." The longer the war lasts the greater the resulting bitterness and hatred.

Last night was quite a busy one with many minor wounded and frostbites coming in. The Huns were counter-attacking around Bastogne and shelled it heavily. Our men though are throwing them back.

We just got a few frostbitten cases. Some arrive barefooted as their feet swell and it becomes impossible to wear shoes. Our "little" litter bearers carry them "piggy back" to the ward. We had to keep men for 2 hours in the Receiving Ward before a bed was vacated by a patient going to the operating room.

I've installed a 2 quart drip bottle in our room. A small faucet is attached to it so we have a "sink-like affair" for washing. The plumbing in the building we live in has been permanently shut off so we draw our water from a Lister bag (32 gallon capacity) in the hallway. The bag often freezes in the unheated corridor. The radiators cannot be repaired so we rely on our stoves for heat. Once more we have to use coke. I've explained to you the difficulties involved in trying to start a fire with coke.

January 5, 1945

About an hour ago 4 soldiers arrived with the story that as they were about to set up in a field someone stepped on a landmine, setting it off and wounding them. These dam Huns mine everything including the wounded. One of the epic stories of the war occurred when the Nazis mined one of our severely wounded soldiers believing him dead. He remained conscious long enough to warn medics not to lift him as he was lying on TNT. After cutting the wires leading to the charge he was rescued. I'm ready to believe anything & everything about the Hun atrocities.

January 8, 1945

The weather is still cloudy, misty and cold. The blanket of snow is gradually increasing. Coal is getting scarce so we must use it sparingly & mix it with the hard to burn coke. Our men have to be for hours in the foxholes. Often wounded can't be reached for hours so they lie there in the snow & cold. The medics though do their best to try to evacuate them sooner.

January 11, 1945

The cold is increasing; this morning was one of the coldest. The entire countryside is covered with a few inches of snow. I believe that in Belgium where the heaviest fighting is now taking place, the snow is heavy. The cold is causing more trouble than the bullets & shells.

January 12, 1945

The hectic rush of the past few days has eased up. Last night I therefore, went to our movies to see "What a Woman". I needed some relaxation and besides, the title reminded me of you, dearie. I've never suffered through a picture so. The cold was intense and my feet were just numb…

The hall which we use as a theater has broken windows, damaged inner-roof and no heat. If sitting for 1 ½ hours in a building can cause your feet to feel frozen just imagine what a foxhole will do.

Most of the wounded we get have been hit by German shells. The Nazi infantry doesn't seem to want to fight at close range. They wait for their big guns to stop the Americans. These Huns have plenty of big stuff.

January 13, 1945

Many of our casualties have been paratroopers and airborne troops (Glider Infantry). We really are proud of them for they're a tough lot, excellent fighters and ready for the worst. Many of them have asked me to return them to duty as soon as possible as their outfit needs them. Coming from a front-line soldier I can appreciate such spirit and morale. These young men are veterans of some tough campaigns.

I am glad to see that the number of casualties has greatly fallen off. In general, the tremendous rush of the past few days is over. We had to keep many patients on litters during the busy days & nights as we had no more cots. The soldiers didn't mind it for as they said: "a litter is a luxury compared to sleeping in a foxhole."

I'm having nightly feasts with all the salamis, chocolates, cookies, etc. I've received.

It seems like ages since I last held you in my arms; since I last had the joys and pleasures of family life; since I last caressed my children. Every night I lie in my bed-roll and dream, for in dreams the world becomes my own. Soon the stark reality appears and all the current brutalities manifest themselves. However, our inevitable victory will make my dreams come true.

January 16, 1945

The incoming casualties are bringing further news of our successful counter attack which is gradually pushing the Huns back. I suppose you read about the 101st Airborne Division... These are the men who held Bastogne against 3 armored German Divisions. They fought and won over tremendous odds because they used excellent tactics. Nazi PWs are astounded at their stand and say that they've never seen anything like it, even on the Russian front.

January 18, 1945

The Huns are retreating and those PWs we treat here are glad that the war is over for them. When you talk to them they give the old line: they're the small men who must obey the order to bear arms, have not committed atrocities, usually admit that the Jews have been mistreated, and are not mixed up in German politics. When asked why they continue fighting when they realize that their cause is a lost one, they reply they must as they are forced.

January 20, 1945

I had visited a PW enclosure a few afternoons ago. Until recently the enclosure was set up in tents, now it occupies buildings. Those prisoners who are needed for questioning are placed in ground floor compartments; privates, non-commissioned officers and officers have their separate compartments. Hay is placed on the floor and the PWs sleep on the warm hay. It was not cold in these compartments; at least they were dry & conducive to sleep.

The interrogations are done by specially trained linguists who know their stuff cold. The valuable information they collect often saves us lives and time. I sat in during some of these interrogations. Of special significance was the typical Nazi mentality as expressed by a German officer candidate --- "I continue fighting because it is my duty; and besides, I can't imagine myself as a slave-worker should we lose."

The Huns never perceived that perhaps someday they might have to answer for their atrocities. They felt perfectly at ease when they enslaved the people of the conquered countries. Yet the Germans expected to get away with their cruelties. Now when they see the handwriting on the wall they suddenly can't imagine themselves tasting their own medicine.

Yesterday afternoon 2 men dressed completely as American soldiers came to our headquarters. One spoke French, the other remained silent. Their story was that they were Frenchmen who had worked for one of our infantry units and were now trying to get a ride to Luxembourg. They were told to return in the morning when one of our vehicles might make the trip. They left, went over to a farmer and asked for food & lodging. The alert farmer was suspicious of their French accent so he stalled them & called some nearby soldiers.

Soon a U.S. soldier returned them to our headquarters where their bags were searched and found to contain quantities of American cigarettes, chocolates, K & C rations and an American pistol & carbine. These men then claimed that the infantry unit they had worked for had paid them in kind. Since this is against Army regulations we became very suspicious. Besides, it is a court-martial offense for soldiers to pay civilians in U.S. weapons which are critical.

Their papers were in order and they even had a note signed by a Major to help them. We know from experience that the Huns have forged many documents. These men were therefore, turned over to the MPs who investigated and found them to be Germans --- probably spies. Remember what I wrote you about the Nazi dirty tricks & how they dressed in American uniforms during the latest offensive.

January 22, 1945

As I write this my memory wanders back to this night just 4 years ago, when you, Mother and the others bid me good-bye at Grand Central where I boarded the Pullman to Madison Barracks. Then my mind was saturated with military questions so in the excitement I perhaps acted like "Alice in Wonderland".

By now I've had 4 years of arrivals and departures. Each arrival being a happier one for I was returning to my sweetheart who had become dearer and dearer to me. Then too, the little treasures you bore me was like a tonic. By the same token, each departure was sadder and became harder to bear.

During my military career my domestic bliss revealed itself by its absence. That which I had accepted as just another comfort was no more; that love and devotion that I had taken for granted as just another matrimonial tradition was missing. I began to feel lonely and forlorn. I began to realize what your presence meant to me; how you gave me a meaning to life; how despondent your absence made me.

Now more than ever I know where my happiness and contentment will begin. You're dearer than ever to me; I love you more than ever and only your presence can and will restore joy and tranquility to my life. It's to you and our two daughters that I offer my love and life for only our reunion will change my present existence to real living.

January 26, 1945

On January 23rd I had completed four years of active service with the Army. To sort of lighten up our existence, I gave a party in our room. About 25 officers & nurses were crowded into our quarters.

A table containing lots of hard candies, chocolates, etc., plus my liquor ration --- bottle of scotch & 2 bottles of champagne --- was set. My roommates contributed much of their "nascherei" which we have in overabundance.

As all were assembled, I commenced giving a resume of my Army career. I carefully blended my comedy with popular songs which all sang. Pretty soon I had the audience rocking with laughter. For over three hours I presented skits & monologues. The audience howled, laughed, danced, sang, drank and became merrier. All present sang to me, "For he's a jolly good fellow" and called it the best party given in our unit. So that ended a few hours of diversions and relaxation.

I hope my 5th year in the Army will see the end of the war. All I care for, after victory, is to return to you, to make a real blue heaven for my family.

January 28, 1945

I had occasion to be in 3 homes in the nearby town. The rooms were low ceiling, small and cold. The elderly tailor-couple told me that while the Nazis were here they would take away lots of furniture for their barracks; they merely entered a house and took what they wanted.

January 30, 1945

Well we've moved again; this time to Belgium --- so now our hospital is somewhere in Belgium. Our nurses traveled in ambulances while most of the officers were in trucks. Everyone had numb feet.

I wore cotton hose over which was worn woolen hose. In addition to the shoes, I wore galoshes, but the feet were freezing. Actually, we needed an artic type of boot. When we reached our destination I found it rather painful to walk. After some exercise my paws limbered up. I can appreciate how easy one can get frostbitten feet in a cramped foxhole.

The snow is deep in Belgium. We passed through some beautiful country which was the scene of bitter and bloody fighting. The heavy snow covered much of the wreckage and devastation.

February 1, 1945

We're getting busy and with the limited space at our disposal the wards are overcrowded. In an effort to prevent frostbitten feet, the Army has introduced a new type of water-proof, high-top shoe. As yet it's too early to say whether the results will be satisfactory.

February 5, 1945

Out here the weather is much warmer. In fact all the snow has melted and our area is again full of mud. Every time we go across the road to the mess hall we trudge in 3 inches of mud. Best of all is that the water tanks don't freeze.

We have no showers here so if one wants to bathe your helmet becomes the bathtub. I therefore, take my sponge in 2 installments. One night I wash from the belly button down and the following night from the navel up. The water is cold, but refreshing.

Irv and I are finally settled in our small, but cozy room. The radiator works so we don't have to mess around with a stove. My bottle contraption gives us running water. We draw water from the water-trailer, carry it in, fill the bottle & wash. There's no closet in the room, but we've rigged up a cross-bar on which our coats, etc. could be hung.

You'd be surprised how one learns to live on makeshift comforts. True we haven't any soft chairs, lounges, etc. I don't miss them anymore. Even such re- freshments as Cokes and ice-cream don't bother me. I miss only fresh milk & its products.

An evacuation hospital doesn't have the conveniences and refinements found in station or general hospitals so to add to our patients' comfort we try to impro- vise items like throat irrigators, steam inhalators, etc.

February 12, 1945

Today your package containing the 2 salamis came. I also received another package from my sister… It contained a salami, mustard… I now have 7 whole salamis and half of one so I hope I don't get any more packages for awhile. I even have enough cookies. Don't send anything until further notice.

Our showers went into operation in a tent so I took advantage of it.

February 15, 1945

I've just finished my evening rounds. It's 10:30 pm and since I'm the Med. O.D. I'm on call. We get a variety of cases... Often our men must cross creeks and streams in order to attack. They've been issued a new type of water-proof boot, but often the streams are higher than the top of the boot so that the feet get wet and cold. Since it's often impossible to change or dry socks in combat, trench foot results. In addition, foxholes are wet at this time of the year. Our men have told me that in most of the pillboxes captured from the Huns they've found sets of silverware from French and Belgium districts. The Nazis robbed these people of their silverware for their own greedy use. A nearby farmer told Irv that during the Ardennes offensive the Huns slaughtered 9 of his cows without compensating him for his cattle.

February 18, 1945

The days continue in their monotonous routine, but we are secure in the knowledge that every day passed is one nearer victory. Sick and wounded arrive, are treated and evacuated. Each case is a grim reminder of what many people don't realize and that is that battles are won by sweat and blood, sacrifice and superhuman effort. My unit has been authorized to wear 3 bronze service stars which indicate that we've supported & participated in 3 major campaigns, the battle for Normandy, the battle for Northern France and the 1st campaign in the battle for Germany. At present the returning mud prevents our tanks from operating effectively. One good frost might give us the break for the Nazis are always looking for time.

February 21, 1945

Since there's been a lull these past few days we could relax a bit by taking an hour's stroll through the picturesque Ardennes Forest.

I walked through the woods which had been a battle-ground a few weeks ago. Under the dense pine trees we could see elaborate dugouts constructed by the Germans. The walls and roofs were supported by logs; the floors were covered with hay. In there they probably managed to keep warm. Scattered all over were Nazi equipment and at about a distance of 100 yards were the American positions. The Huns were dug in for defense whereas the Americans merely dug plain foxholes for the offensive. Many shrapnel pieces were lying about. If you can imagine various sized, jagged edged pieces of steel, flying at tremendous speed you can conjecture artillery wounds.

After the stroll I felt refreshed and returned to my patients. Amongst them were 2 officers who had been captured by the Germans during our counter-offensive. One was a Med. Officer and the other an Infantry Officer. Their story is a very interesting one. Not only does it relate their adventures, but brings out the barbarism of the Nazis.

While the Germans were retaking a small village the Med. Officer remained to care for one of our seriously wounded officers whose leg had been blown off. He wasn't permitted to stay by the casualty, but was taken to the German interrogator. Later on the Huns told him that the severely wounded officer had died, but I wouldn't be surprised if they gave him the Nazi finishing touch.

Near the front lines the Med. Officer was treated fairly well. The interrogator promised him preferential treatment such as notifying his family by short wave radio that although captured he's safe & well, etc. The Med. Officer was a veteran, knew all the Nazi chicanery and false promises so he stood pat and only gave his name, rank and serial number which is in accordance with the Geneva Convention concerning PWs.

The tortures commenced when he was removed to a collecting point for prisoners. Here the Americans were kept from a few days to a few weeks and then moved farther into Germany. The Germans fed the American PWs, both officers & men, hard black bread, a loaf per 6 men, and a thick soup made with potato peelings --- the potatoes were eaten only by the Nazi soldiers --- and when the water had boiled some ersatz flour was mixed. Sometimes they cooked it with some horsemeat or horse liver, but most always removed the meat before serving time and gave it to the Nazis. The soup tasted like paste and most of the Americans couldn't eat it. Our men couldn't eat that hard black bread and tried to sort of toast it.

The men therefore, grew weaker from such starvation rations. The coarseness of these meager and poorly prepared foods caused diarrhea which increased the progressive weakening. The Geneva Convention provides that prisoners of war are to be furnished the same rations as one's own troops. A Nazi is always ready to complain, never to comply.

Our men are not supplied with even one blanket or hay or straw. They are crowded into a room, unheated and often wet or leaking. Many developed frostbitten feet and despite the fact that their feet are swollen, blistered and black and blue they are forced to work repairing their roads, digging gun emplacements, carrying ammunition or doing some of the hard work of the camp. Again the Geneva Convention of which Germany is a signatory prohibits the use of PWs for combat work.

On the average 4 men died each day from starvation, overwork, mistreatment, exhaustion & exposure. The guards often beat our men who fell at their work. After our planes bombed the nearby town some of the German civilian men would come out with sticks and beat our soldiers who were working under guard nearby. The Nazi guard would permit this.

Once about 14 of our men were wounded during a bombing raid. The Nazis merely bandaged them, had them carried to the room and left to die. No Red Cross representative is permitted to enter or visit such torture chambers. The Huns say that these are temporary camps and that deep in Germany are the real PW camps.

The sanitary facilities are abominable. No provisions are made for safe drinking water. The latter is merely scooped out of the mud or ditches. There are no washing utilities; toilets are merely foxholes. After dusk our men cannot use the outside toilet or rather hole and since there are no inside toilet facilities, you can imagine the rest. If our men haven't their own helmets or tin cans to keep the soup in they are out of luck as the Huns won't furnish any utensil. Either one borrows a can or helmet from his buddy or gets nothing at all. Cigarettes are also denied them.

When I compare this with our treatment of the supermen PWs I become enraged. We even inject the wounded Nazis with the precious Penicillin. Even in our transient PW stockades the Nazis are given substantial food.

February 24, 1945

Amongst my patients I was called to see was a 51 years old German woman evacuated from one of the German towns our troops had captured. I asked her whether she had any objections to being treated by a Jewish doctor. "Oh no"! she replied. "I never did mind." But perhaps your Fuehrer might mind? To which she made a denouncing gesture of Hitler.

February 26, 27, 1945

Today is an important day in our lives for it's your birthday, the day you were born for me. I'm alone with my thoughts of you, hoping and praying that soon we shall be reunited to celebrate all blessed events together.

Tomorrow will be our 7th Anniversary and for the fourth time we're apart. May it be the last time for I want you more than ever. I long for you and the kids; I wish for an end of this dreadful existence, this monotonous being. May our next Anniversary see us together for keeps.

A few days ago I rode in a jeep to Liege, Belgium, a city of about 400,000. The roads are pretty bad in spots so we got quite a bouncing. The destruction of the recent Ardennes Battle was everywhere along the roads & villages.

The people are quite friendly. Their hatred of the Germans appears genuine. A woman storekeeper told me that her husband was taken away and forced to work in Hamburg for the past 5 years. The Huns didn't hesitate to rob the Belgians of food, etc. The Huns committed many atrocities against the Belgians during the fatal counter-offensive in the Ardennes.

I had my radio fixed and it plays well now. You should have heard me try to converse with these people few of whom understand English or German. In one store I asked the lady whether she had an English-French dictionary. I got what I wanted by pointing to the word.

February 28, 1945

It is midnight now and I've had a most busy day as we were suddenly swamped with cases. Many of them were casualties from booby-traps and land mines. Many of the patients now are between 19 — 25 years of age who've recently reached the continent.

We'll probably set up in tents in our next move as most of the buildings ahead have been destroyed.

March 2, 1945

I was quite busy these past few days and today has been the first lull. There's so much to do and so little time that we just rush to get the cases in shape for evacuation and thereby have room for the new patients.

So the empty days pass in review. Actually, they serve as a review of our life --- so long married, so little time together; yet 2 lovely daughters and so much to look forward to. Until we meet again, all my love.

March 6, 1945

I must travel as light as possible so I'm returning all your letters for safekeeping. When I'll accumulate more they'll likewise be returned to you. Perhaps in our old age we'll want to reread our correspondence.

From now on…no packages until further notice. I've got too much canned foods, etc. to lug around.

March 7, 1945

Now that we are resting for a few days preparatory to the soon anticipated rush we were given passes to Brussels, capital of Belgium… A truck loaded with nurses & officers left at 7 a.m. It was a rainy and windy day and the bouncing along many of the poor roads wasn't exactly to our comfort. We finally reached this city…and had about 6 hours to shop and go sightseeing.

The prices are highway robbery. We get 44 Belgium francs for a dollar and are paid in such francs. Some Belgiums openly request American bills and will pay twice as much or more for it. I have a hunch that American currency is sold on the black market and smuggled to the Nazis who in turn try to get dollar bills to pay for their espionage activities in the U.S. or South America. The Huns can afford to pay such fantastic prices for dollars since they robbed these people so heavily & counterfeited their money.

Brussels is noted for its lace, but nowadays our soldiers consider the city notorious for its chiseling. To the civilians the magic word "American" denotes money so prices are sky high. In one store the woman asked me 125 francs for a small piece of lace. I sort of took the label out of her hand and noticed it marked as 75 francs. She said that, that was a mistake. I did buy a few items of lacework. I'll mail these to you tomorrow...

Brussels is a rest center for the British and Canadian Armies and until one week ago was not used by the Americans. The Canadians have established a gift shop for their troops, a sort of Post Exchange and that's what the American Army should do. Then the civilian merchants would stop plundering as we'd buy gifts in our own store. The Canadians also have a 2 hour sightseeing tour of the city. It's free to all uniformed Allied personnel. At some points we got out of the car and walked. The Palace of Justice building is a huge, beautiful, dome-shaped structure which took 17 years to build and was completed in 1883.

Before the Nazis left Brussels --- I believe it was last Sept. --- they set the building on fire. Belgian firemen who tried to intervene were shot at. Since the building is of stone they only managed to destroy the inside.

All Jews had to wear a yellow "Star of David" on their jackets & overcoats. The black market was actually controlled by the Nazis and only the quislings or the rich had enough to eat. The guide further added that most Jews were taken away; all younger Belgians had to go to Germany to slave.

There are quite a few 1940, 1941 models of American automobiles... The guide added that during the German occupation such cars were hidden as the Huns would seize it for their own use. Now the Belgians use them, but where they get the gas is a mystery. Of course, they could buy it on the black market which steals it from the American Army.

Shady characters roam the streets trying to sell you cognac or human merchandise. They ask you in English "Want nice girls" and then try to lead you to a café where the association of pimp, whore and owner reek the harvest of your money. Our Army has already had some deaths from the denatured alcohol and the so-called "homebrew drinks" that were sold to soldiers.

It rained and continued drizzling all day. We had a very bumpy ride home which we reached about 11 p.m. To get away from the woods and mud even for a few hours is perhaps worth all the trouble of 7 – 8 hours ride in a truck.

March 8, 1945

The news is excellent. The radio has announced the establishment of an American bridgehead across the formidable Rhine River. From secret sources we knew this a day before the radio made the announcement.

Once this bridgehead is extended the final battle for Germany will begin and I believe end in good time. We have no illusions as we know it'll be a tough fight. For us here the European war won't be over until the last Nazi soldier surrenders.

March 14, 1945

Greetings again, but this time from inside Germany… I couldn't send you letters sooner as we were on the move & naturally there's no postal service during such a time. Our Air Force did a fine supporting job and if the Nazis had any sense they'd call it quits now instead of destroying & wrecking most of Germany. Patients are arriving fast so we'll all be very busy.

March 15, 1945

The weather is cool & brisk; the mornings are rather cold. We have no heat in the rooms. The hospital we're occupying was run by nuns. I was called by the Colonel to translate as we were conducted through the building. As I gaze at the ruins of this city I'm thankful that Americans are spared such scenes. This city feels like a cemetery --- only a handful of civilians are around. Of course, there's no fraternization.

March 17, 1945

A captured German said that the Americans made the mistake of not cleaning out the civilians from the towns for some of them not only hide Nazi soldiers, but also snipe at our troops. There have actually been cases where German civilians have killed our men. I guess we easy going Americans are still suckers. The conquered countries know better.

March 23, 1945

Our hospital is so full that we must keep patients in the hallways before they get their turn to the operating room. Many Huns have been admitted to our hospital and as usual most of them proclaim their innocence. An enlisted man told me that a Colonel in his outfit was wounded & 2 med-aid men were trying to carry him back on a litter. The Germans were shooting at them so the Colonel ordered the medics to place him near a tree, take off & return later. When they did return with more help they found this Colonel dead; he had been riddled with a German tommy at close range. The Huns must have walked up to him & let loose.

March 25, 1945

Yesterday afternoon I walked out for a ½ hour and wandered into the Catholic Church... The irony of it was to see American Catholic soldiers and officers, with their guns, attending the services in one section while the German civilians prayed in a nearby section, praying together, the Americans for their cause and the Germans for their own. I'm still busy and since we're moving fast I guess our hospital will also let loose to keep pace with General Patton. The German civilians try to fraternize, but we know the price. An American Warrant Officer...was court-martialed and fined $390 for fraternizing.

March 29, 1945

Greetings from deep inside Germany for yesterday our outfit crossed the formidable Rhine River into the eastern part of Germany. We were proud to pass through German villages, towns and cities. There was, of course, no waving or cheering; the superfolks either stared at us or looked away. Our hospital is back in tents now and once more we have four to a tent. With our past experience we can certainly make it fairly comfortable. We found lots of Nazi lumber and are using it to good advantage. We are quite glad to be so deep inside Germany and once and for all show these super-duper butchers that the U.S. & Allied Armies are their superiors.

March 30, 1945

It is now almost 8 p.m. and after a busy day I'm back in my tent writing this letter by candlelight. The hospital proper has electricity, but our living quarters have none. Perhaps the latter will be wired in a few days.

As I write the artillery is blasting away. At some points we are not far away from the front. The battle ground at present is so shifting that what may be the front now is the zone of the interior tomorrow.

Our hospital is set up in the outskirts of a town in a wooded area. Our Army is moving so fast that we are not getting too many casualties. We did get many American soldiers who had been captured by the Nazis and rescued by one of our armored divisions. I wish the people back home could have seen these half-starved, lice-infested American soldiers --- or else could have listened to their sad tales. Perhaps then would the "pampering" of the Nazi prisoners in America stop.

These American soldiers were crowded into boxcars (freight trains) until there was not much room left. A pail was set in a corner & served as a latrine. They were forced to march most of the way into the interior of Germany. The food was atrocious & so little that most of them were semi-starved. About 400 men were crowded into a big room and were forced to sleep two to a bunk. The latter were 3 tiers high. Each pair was given a filthy, lousy blanket so it is no won-der that they were full of lice, scratches & sores. Most of them were forced to work hard even when sick & feverish. The guards would beat them if they didn't.

They received no Red Cross packages despite the fact that the American Red Cross sends each American prisoner a weekly food package. One of my officer patients told me that after capturing a German town they entered a house & found 4 cans of skimmed milk labeled "American Red Cross". When questioned, this German family said their officials had issued it to them.

Last night was the second Seder. We were supplied with 6 boxes of matzos and a quart of wine. I conducted the Seder and our Protestant Chaplain delivered a fine sermon.

Lest I forget, amongst the rescued American soldiers who were prisoners of the Germans were some Jewish men. One told me that a British Tommy told him to state his religion as Protestant as the Huns were hard on Jewish PWs. They made these Hebrews pick-up unexploded bombs.

We are quite optimistic now for we believe that the Huns are at the end of their rope. Of course, we are not like the radio commentators, who not being here & not having to fight this war, can chatter all they want. There are still a few hard battles, but the end may come anytime as they are being badly licked.

April 3, 1945

Our hospital has the distinction of being the first 3rd Army Evacuation Hospital to cross the Rhine. We are receiving many American and British soldiers & officers former prisoners in Germany. I'm really sorry that people back home can't see them or hear their hair-raising stories.

April 5, 1945

In this set-up captured German PWs are sent to my wards. Recently I got a Nazi Lt. Col & 1st Lt., both doctors. With their usual Nazi "sweetest" they tried to tell me that they treat captured Americans like their own men. Just at this time I had a bunch of our soldiers, former PWs of the Germans, starved & sick, some with pneumonia. I told the supermen off so they finally said that the Germans haven't the food. This remark enraged me & I replied "You brutes are always bellyaching about the Geneva Red Cross Treaty governing the treatment of prisoners. The treaty demands equality of food for PWs which means same as your own troops get. Do you feed your men bread & water? I don't see you losing 50 lbs. You & the other Nazi troops don't look undernourished." To this they had nothing to say. The Huns have purposely starved or underfed our captured soldiers, beaten them, let them die. These are not propaganda stories, but true facts.

April 9, 1945

Since we are old timers we don't mind living in tents. We've managed to rig up a lot of conveniences and our field showers certainly are a great source of comfort and relaxation.

Being in Germany is like being in jail. We can't fraternize with the Huns & may talk to them only on official business. This is really an excellent policy and will show the Huns that this time we mean business.

Many Germans deny that they knew about the atrocities. Perhaps they are right, but as a nation the Germans have committed crimes that befit barbarians and not a so-called civilized nation. It'll be over soon & the curse of this century will be liquidated & I hope forever.

April 12, 1945

A few USO shows and one G.I. show were presented to our patients and personnel and some of the performances were quite good. We have frequent movies, but some of these pictures are so bad that many of us leave early.

I've been to a large German city & saw the effects of the bombing. It's no wonder that the German civilians are glad that their cities are in our hands for this spares them such terrible ordeals. The rubble is piled high and removed from the streets which appear clean. Some big cities have really gotten the works --- a tribute to the efficiency of the Allied Air Force. The Huns in the captured cities hear planes, look skywards and appear relieved as our bombers head towards the still uncaptured cities.

April 13, 1945

Early this morning our radio announced the tragic news of the sudden death of President Roosevelt. It was a great shock and regret to all of us for a man of his caliber is scarce. Amongst our officers the majority wish that the policies of FDR be continued.

April 16, 1945

Our hospital is taking it easy now so we have plenty of chances to make short trips to some of the nearby towns. Yesterday we walked about 5 miles to a town where a large German factory was producing airplane motors. Our Air Force gave it a good licking. The Hun civilians stared at us as we proudly strolled by & tried to cater to our wishes. Of course, it's all artificial as they hope to gain something like candy, cigarettes, food, etc. Our Army prohibits any kind of fraternization … Now most of them plead innocence. In one of their recently captured camps 400 foreign "slaves" were found shot through the head.

I had the pleasure of walking through the big city of Frankfurt on the Main River. About half of the town is permanently destroyed. One just has to see it for himself to visualize the terrific ordeal of a bombing. People stand in long lines before food stores which ration out certain foods. We entered one of the few open camera stores where only some films and photo accessories are to be bought. I did the talking for the group & the storekeeper was exceedingly cautious. During the sale she remarked that she had enough of the war.

April 21, 1945

We're again in a new location after a long trip through some very scenic German landscapes. Some of the big cities…were so badly destroyed that in some sections of these cities not a house or building remained. The towns we passed through had white flags hanging from their windows. Truck loads of captured Germans passed us on the road & some German civilians waved to them, but looked at us with poker faces. The new area is very picturesque and should the weather remain propitious our present field will be very satisfactory. It can't last long now.

April 22, 1945

We are now set-up in our new location and expect to receive casualties today. Advance reports indicate that the American casualties are not heavy so we hope it will continue so.

Our living quarters (tents) aren't wired, as yet, for electricity so we use candles. Last night was spent in our tent, sitting & talking about home & our children. The candles made a dreary atmosphere.

On every German road one can see people of every nationality carrying or carting their meager possessions and trying to return to their own land. The Army calls these ex-slave workers "displaced persons" and has established camps for them.

We passed a few such establishments where mothers were taking care of their children, washing clothes, etc. The Allied policy is to gather these hundreds of thousands, or perhaps millions of displaced persons into camps and sort them. After that they are, if possible, returned to their native country.

These ex-slave-workers --- and that's really what the Nazis used them for --- are a great problem to our officials. Some of these displaced persons roam around, steal and have even broken into captured Nazi food warehouses and stolen hundreds of canned foods which our Army was saving for distribution to these very people. These people have been oppressed for so long that they go wild with their sudden freedom.

Our Army has captured so much German equipment that is usable that everyone has something. Looting is strictly prohibited, but any item of the German Army becomes the property of the U.S. Army which may then dispose of it in any manner.

The German civilians seem to be well dressed and not undernourished. Their children aren't as malnourished as those of the occupied countries. The Nazi Army lacked little, except gasoline. The latter seems to be the reason why the Luftwaffe makes infrequent appearances. At times, some German planes attack our front-line troops, but by now the Luftwaffe is a legend.

We're about to win the European War so our reunion can't be too far off.

April 24, 1945

We've been having inclement weather since arriving in this new area, heavy rains which have begun to turn this field into areas of mud. The bright spot here is that our tent quarters have electric lights. My radio can therefore, operate and once more the dreariness of candle lights has been turned into the brightness of electricity plus the enjoyment & relaxation of radio. We have captured a nearby factory which contained large boards of plywood so now all of us have them under our cots & this helps keep our shoes, etc. dry as the ground gets quite damp.

April 27, 1945

I sure share your descriptive sentiments and indeed realize what our separation has meant for both of us. I too yearn for you & the children, for our home, for the quiet of peace and the normal life. Yet there is satisfaction, much gratification in the knowledge that I'm doing my bit where I'm needed, backing up my countrymen, our gallant soldiers. Whenever any of us get blue and lonely, just think of the battlefield and what some men are enduring. For our present burdens our future lives will become brighter and richer.

April 30, 1945

Not far from us is a PW enclosure where many thousands of Germans are kept in a guarded field until transportation becomes available for their evacuation to the rear. I had a Russian Lt. who had been a German prisoner for 3 years. He worked in German coal mines & said that the Nazis treated Russian officers worse than Russian soldiers … He added that Russian officers & soldiers of Jewish extraction were killed by the Huns. Other Russians were made to undress, tied to stakes in the ground & cold water was poured on them until they froze to death (in winter – for summer they had other means of death).

May 2, 1945

I was glad that Laura enjoyed her birthday party so much. I always want our children to celebrate happy occasions no matter where their Daddy might be.

The radio has just announced the death of Hitler. That called for a celebration. We must make sure though that this isn't a Nazi hoax to enable the Fuehrer to escape to a hideout and perhaps continue his nefarious works.

On certain sectors our men are encountering some stiff resistance; in others the opposition is light. We aren't receiving many casualties, but continue admitting a goodly number of medical cases.

I guess you are well aware that we're deep inside Germany so that most of us have seen much of naziland. As I travel from town to town and city to city the terrific destruction by our air bombings is apparent everywhere.

It will take years to rebuild and erase such piles of debris and rubble. Germans are seen everywhere searching amidst the ruins. In woods they gather firewood. Long lines of people are always present in front of food stores. As soon as our troops vacate an area German civilians are around to rummage through the leftovers.

In the newer conquered districts the Germans are timid and most cooperative. This attitude is also reflected in the children. Once the latter get accustomed to our troops they try to play up by cheering, waving, making the V sign and even throwing flowers.

As I gaze at such horrors of destruction & disruption I think of how much more terrible the next war might be. I am so glad that my loved ones did not have to endure such ordeals. Words are inadequate to describe the horrors and sufferings of war; one must see it --- and once seen it is never forgotten.

I haven't seen, as yet, some of the Nazi concentration and extermination camps. Some of the soldiers who've seen the grim and ghastly scenes are chilled & numbed to the realization that this century & civilization have produced such barbarians. When one considers such bestialities it becomes plain that the so-called innocent Germans who tolerated Nazism & even applauded it aren't even getting half of their own brand of medicine. No, the poor Germans didn't object when millions of slave- workers were torn away from their families & forced to slave for the German nation.

This evening the radio announced that the German Army in Italy had surrendered unconditionally. Unless my hunch is wrong I believe that the Huns in Germany will soon surrender --- perhaps you'll be reading this letter after V-E Day.

May 7, 1945

Meanwhile, the radio had been reporting that Churchill would most likely announce V-E Day within the ensuing 24 – 48 hours. Our men were busier taking prisoners than fighting. The Huns were surrendering in hundreds of thousands. Large fields were fenced in with barbed wire and the Nazi soldiers packed in. One of the PW fields near us contained about 40,000 prisoners who had very little room to maneuver. They were fed cans of "C" Rations twice daily. As soon as trucks were available the Nazis were packed in and carted away to regular PW camps. If you'd ever seen or know the way the Huns treated the Allied soldiers you'd say they're being too well treated here.

Early this morning we packed, loaded and mounted the trucks for the 18th time since landing in Normandy. We were to travel about 110 miles to our new destination towards the Czechoslovakian border.

On the way we passed the same scenes of destruction, but as we neared the Czech border the towns and villages showed less & less destruction. It was mountainous country with all its rugged beauty. Almost every house & public building hung a white flag as a token of surrender.

Many truckloads of liberated French soldiers & slaves passed us & we greeted each other enthusiastically. Many Slav worker slaves (Russians, Poles, Yugoslavs, etc.) who had evidently been newly liberated walked along the road. They were a sorry looking lot, emaciated & poorly dressed. Many saluted us when they noticed our officers' insignia. We threw them chocolates, cigarettes & food and they thanked us. These unfortunates appeared so pitiful and forlorn. They should be allowed to take care of the Germans --- they remember.

We passed another outfit which gave us the cheering news that V - E Day was announced. We cheered and cheered.

As we entered the town near where we were to bivouac we saw armed German soldiers riding motorcycles, trucks & even tanks. We learned ... that the Nazis had surrendered and that the entire German 11th Armored division was driving into this pre-arranged area to surrender. The rumor was that General

Patton had even supplied them with enough gas to enable these gasless vehicles to reach the surrender assembly point.

Well, I've related enough. The terrible European War is now over. Our victory is complete and we hope, a lasting one. There are many rumors here as to our future. As soon as I learn something definite I'll inform you. In the interim rest assured that the worst is over now and that it won't be long before we'll embrace each other. Everyone is celebrating here so I'll join them.

May 9, 10, 1945

Here we are camped in a German field near the Czechoslovakian border, with real spring days, pretty scenery and nothing to do. In a few days though we'll move into Czechoslovakia and set up as a station hospital.

Yesterday I took a long ride in with our mail truck to Pilsen, Czechoslovakia, the home of the great armament industry, the Skoda Works. As we passed through... the Czech towns we were greeted like conquering heroes. It was reminiscent of our passage through France when the fervor was sky high.

As our truck passed a newly liberated town we saw a scene that made us stop & dismount. About 20 men and 4 women were lined up against a fence with their backs to the crowd and their hands up.

Since most of the Czechs speak some German I learned the following pertinent facts: The ... 24 people were Germans who had been active on behalf of the Nazis, had caused Czechs to be shot or sent to concentration camps. A day before the town was liberated these Nazis had hidden SS Nazi troops in their homes & spied for them. The Czech who walked around as the main guard had been a prisoner in the notorious Buchenwald Concentration Camp. He therefore, had the bitter memory of 3 ½ years Nazi torture and remembered well all the Nazi tricks.

With a stick he walked around banging those whose hands were slowly dropping on the bare head, hands & neck. Huns immediately raised their arms higher. Then he'd make one of them bend over and force the adjoining Hun to whip him. If the whipping wasn't forceful enough the guards would beat them. The Huns had to alternate the process. The 4 women were made to do the same.

Perhaps it wasn't a pleasant sight...., but these brutal Huns were responsible for the most fiendish atrocities and the poor enslaved peoples of the occupied countries were only giving the Nazis a mild dose of their own medicine.

May 11, 1945

We moved yesterday to Pilsen, Czechoslovakia and have again set up our hospital in a field. The weather is grand and we're all anxious to see sights, so as soon as I see my last patient I'll go to town with my friends.

May 12, 1945

I took a walk through the town yesterday. The famous Skoda Works employed about 14,000 people and many foreigners were forced by the Nazis to slave there 12 hours daily. Our Air Force had however, given it a good going over.

One hardly sees stout natives or children. The Nazis saw to that. In my wards are American & British soldiers who had been in German captivity for 6 months. The Huns let them loose a few days ago and told them to make their way to the American lines as best they could. All were very undernourished, some seriously ill, with swollen bodies. They were awakened at 5 a.m., given a thin turnip soup & black bread for breakfast, then marched for 4 miles to work – no lunch – marched back at 6 p.m., fed soup, coffee & black bread. Each man was given ¾ lb. bread daily. He could carry it to work & eat it at noon, if he desired. I wish all back home could see the broken bodies of our men.

May 15, 1945

We don't have any more edible garbage. The Czechs & liberated flood around our kitchens to devour all our leftovers; no sooner is it brought out than they begin to grab. Some consume it on the spot, others collect it.

Last Sunday an English-speaking Czech acted as our guide. Our trucks took us to a 14th century castle, about 18 miles from Pilsen. Only the thick outer walls are left. We climbed to the top and got an excellent glimpse of the Bohemian forest and countryside. This guide impressed upon us the extent of the Nazi operations of oppression & cruelties during the 6 years of the German occupation. Near this ancient castle is a small inn which had no beer, but served some type of orangeade. The proprietor refused money so we gave him some cigarettes & chocolates.

Almost every American has struck up civilian acquaintances who visit our hospital daily. Last evening a Czech couple visited me. I took them to see a movie which our unit was showing. It was the first American picture they had seen in over 6 years. The Nazis used to tell them that in America people are starving and have very little. The Czechs were rationed one pair of work shoes every 2 years and one pair of social shoes every 3 years --- food of course, was very limited. While the Nazis ate the conquered people were hungry.

May 16, 1945

The point system for discharge has been officially put into effect. It also applies to officers, but there's always the distressing qualifying statement "if the officer is not deemed essential." I have 121 points --- 85 is the minimum, at present. I should therefore, be amongst those very eligible for discharge. If I stay away much longer from you, you might suffer a nervous upset. I want a complete discharge as I've had enough of the Army.

May 20, 1945

During mealtime lines form near our mess tents, full of Czechs and liberated slaves, each with some container, anxiously waiting the distribution of our left-overs. To avoid unruly grabbing we have them form a line. Our cook then gives some food to each one --- as long as it lasts. All civilians pick-up any cigar or cigarette butts they notice.

Today we filled out the points-card. My 121 places me second highest in the outfit. I've indicated my desire… We hope to return to the U.S.A. within 3 months, but you know the Army, it might take longer.

In the meantime think about a possible office location. When I return I hope to take a year's post-graduate course at Columbia Medical School & perhaps hold office hours at night. Under the "G.I. Bill of Rights" the government will pay tuition up to $500 plus allowance of $75 monthly for living expenses. I'm therefore, sure we'll manage. I want the course to specialize in internal medicine, my field.

May 25, 1945

I was invited to a Czech home. I dressed in my so-called class A uniform & went. The last time I wore my dress uniform was in England 11 months ago. The Czechs hope that the Americans will remain for a long time for they prefer us to the Russians. The Yank with his friendliness and gratis distribution of cigarettes, chocolates, etc. is very popular.

I think we're getting another battle star thus raising my point score to 126. You can resume sending me a package a month, especially salamis.

May 27, 1945

Our commanding officer has told us that from what he knows we are to remain in Europe for at least 3 months more. The truth is that no one knows the score as such policies are determined not by the individual armies, but by the War Department & by General Eisenhower's headquarters. There's otherwise not much new here. My ward keeps me occupied. We see movies every night.

May 28, 1945

Yes, I know how lonely your nights must be for I also have experienced and am still experiencing lonely nights. Now that it's over in this theater we're impatient. I'm most anxious to return to civilian life and you. I want to enjoy my children & the home I hardly know. At present all I can do is hope it'll be soon.

A Czech acquaintance showed me a steel whip with which the brutal Nazis used to beat their unfortunate victims. It had a steel knob which could easily crack a skull. I know atrocity tales that would sound fantastic in this day and age.

Last Saturday morning Jewish services were held by the Chaplain who read from a small Torah which had been hidden & preserved by a German Jew in a concentration camp. This Israelite found it in the basement of a building he was forced to work and managed to conceal it in his wretched quarters. Our Jewish Chaplain will take it to America and present it to some synagogue with the name of the man who risked his life to preserve this holy Torah inscribed on it.

May 30, 1945

I'm kept fairly busy with my cases. It's not the quantity, but the types which require complete histories & physical exams. Yesterday I worked 11 hours on a patient who had been a PW of the Germans for 6 months. He had weighed 160 lbs. prior to his captivity. He was brought here very emaciated, body swollen and very anemic. After extensive treatment he improved for 24 hours & then took a turn for the worse and finally expired despite all our efforts. The Germans killed this American boy by starvation just as sure as they killed our soldiers by bullets.

June 10, 1945

Last night a group of us went to the Pilsen Opera House to see the operetta "Polish Blood." After the fine performance…we went to the home of my Czech friend where we sat around & gossiped. As the group talked with each other you could have heard English, Czech and German. The Czech hate to speak the Nazi lingo, but usually must as we can't converse otherwise with those who can't speak English.

June 14, 1945

About 5 nights ago someone broke into Capt. S's tent, stole his cigarettes, chocolates, canned goods & cigars. We have placed a guard around the officers' & nurses' area & kick out all vagrants & kids who often enter our area proper. Food & cigarettes are worth fortunes & the displaced persons or hungry Czech civilians will not hesitate to steal such scarce items.

June 16, 1945

In the evenings when I'm not Medical O.D. I go to the Czech opera or to the Officers' Club in town. This sweating out business is to no one's liking, but if we must stay in Europe we prefer to be here rather than in Germany. We've made friends and almost everyone of us has Czech civilians visiting.

June 26, 1945

We're all anxiously awaiting news of our fate. Our unit is still functioning. When it will be dissolved is anyone's guess. I hope I can get to you soon for I'm tired of everything here.

June 28, 1945

We've been awarded the 4th battle participation star which gives me five more points and brings my present total to 126 points. Another campaign star is still pending and should it be awarded I'll have 5 additional points. The Colonel told us that low point men & officers will be transferred out of this outfit & high point men will replace them. Our unit will probably return to the states with little of the old personnel remaining and it is believed that this will occur in October.

June 30, 1945

I've been talking to a Jewish woman who spent 3 years in a Nazi enforced ghetto in Lodz, Poland and 1 year in a concentration camp. The tales are enough to cause tears.

July 2, 1945

Yesterday afternoon I went with my Czech friends…to the circus. It was a one tent show, mostly acrobats, clowns and a 7 horse act. When some of the acrobats had finished their act they'd walk around selling their picture postcards while the next act was in progress.

July 4, 1945

Our Independence Day is being celebrated in Pilsen with parades & shows. The Czech stores will be closed all day. Last night I saw a U.S. Army stage show. The magician…really was good. It poured the entire evening & night and again our area is full of puddles & mud.

July 8, 1945

We've lost so many officers that I'm Medical O.D. every 5th night. Our commanding officer will leave in a few days, a permanent transfer to a station hospital in Munich. It rained again… Most of our leather goods and canvas (tents) are getting moldy --- a reminder of my Panama days.

This is the last letter I have from my Dad. I can only surmise that he received orders to return to the States, telegraphed my Mother and left Europe as soon as he could.

Czechoslovakia

Captain Cantor in front of his tent Pilsen, Czechoslovakia, June, 1945

Sixteen

I have a very vague memory of standing on a boardwalk holding my Father's hand. I am 4 years old and we are in Rockaway, NewYork. Dad is in an Army uniform. People are lined up and they are all yelling and cheering. Looking back I can only assume that it was August 15, 1945, V-J Day (Victory over Japan Day). World War II was finally, completely over!

Dad entered the Army on January 23, 1941 and was officially discharged on November 17, 1945. The life that had been put on hold for almost five years could finally begin again. Sometime in 1946 our family moved to a large, ground floor apartment on Montgomery Street in Brooklyn, NewYork. Our living quarters and Dad's office were shared until they moved 21 years later to the Sheepshead Bay area of Brooklyn. Dad also rented office space from a doctor in another part of Brooklyn.

Our family grew with the arrival of two more daughters, Irene Sue and Ruth (Candy) Marilyn. It was a busy, happy home. Dad worked very hard to provide for us. My parents put a great emphasis on education. It had been their ticket into the Middle Class. They put all four of their girls through college.

My Father loved being a doctor. For 38 years he cared for and worried about his patients. He was an excellent diagnostician and developed a loyal following. People sometimes *waited patiently for hours to see Dr. Cantor. He did not work by appointment; just listened carefully to each patient and took his time. When he was in his sixties he took classes and passed an exam to become a Diplomate of the American Academy of Family Practice. He was still practicing medicine when he died suddenly at the age of 74.*

Through the years Dad told various war stories, but in typical "kid fashion" I didn't pay too much attention to them. On Friday nights after office hours our small dining room became a place for friends and family to gather. Here my Father would hold court and the group would argue and discuss the politics of the day. One of his old army buddies who lived near-by often joined them.

The pride and honor of serving the country that he loved and caring for its soldiers stayed with Dad throughout his life. He was grateful that he was one of the lucky ones who had returned home. He knew that because of the sacrifices of others, his four daughters and eight grandchildren would inherit a democratic and free America.

Acknowledgements

This project took about a year and a half to do. I would like to recognize and thank all those who encouraged me along the way.

A hug and special thanks to my husband, Carl Zelman, my chief technical man. He was always there to patiently solve all my problems when the computer didn't want to do what I had in mind.

My three sisters --- Sylvia Cohen, Irene Adler and Ruth Reynolds Nikolov --- gave me lots of support. They were eager to get to know our Dad as a young man. They also wanted their children and grandchildren to know this part of our family history. My sister, Sylvia, was a great help in proof reading the initial manuscript.

During the time that I spent organizing and reading the letters, I often related parts of them to my children, their spouses and my grandchildren. Their interest and questions encouraged me to keep working on the book. Thank you to my family --- Eric and Jill Zelman, Tanner and Jack; Jeffrey and Shawn Zelman, Taylor, Sawyer and Skylar; Sharon and Jonathan Chiat, Sydney and Carly. Special thanks to Shawn Zelman for proofing the final manuscript.

Thank you to Joyce Zier, my friend of many years, for the information she gathered for me on publishing.

I am especially indebted to Chuck Cascio for all his help in bringing this book to fruition. He graciously gave me his time, encouragement and lots of valuable advice on how to go about publishing a book.

About the Author

L aura Cantor Zelman is a graduate of Vassar College, where she majored in sociology and minored in English. After graduating she moved to the Washington, D.C. area and eventually settled in Virginia. Here Laura and her husband owned and operated a business together for thirty years.

Born and raised in Brooklyn, New York, she is the oldest of the Cantor siblings. Laura grew up in a vibrant ethnic household, which never shied away from lively political discussion. The Zelman's have three children and seven grandchildren.

She has been a writer for and editor of various volunteer organizations' publications. Laura also enjoys writing songs, poems and skits for family celebrations. This passion acted as the base for Laura's organization and excerpting of the over five hundred letters that comprise *In My Father's Words*.

35167103R00141

Made in the USA
Middletown, DE
21 September 2016